PETERSON   BRAKMO   DAVIE

TCP Congestion Control

A Systems Approach

SYSTEMS APPROACH LLC

Contents

Foreword

Congestion control is unquestionably one of the most important, most fundamental topics in computer networking. It's also one of most challenging, as it requires controlling endpoints that are potentially distributed around the globe, in different organizations, and supporting different applications. The role of the network layer in supporting transport-layer congestion control is also a multi-faceted, nuanced challenge. And congestion control is needed in just about every Internet scenario one can imagine: from the public Internet that spans the globe and carries all types of traffic, to long "fat" pipes carrying massive amounts of file-transfer data, to specialized datacenter networks, to private commercial backbone networks, to mobile and wireless networks.

With all of these challenges, how does one make sense of the many (many!) approaches towards congestion control that have been developed? What are the fundamental challenges these approaches are solving? What is the role of the network layer, and more broadly what is the design space for congestion control protocols? Are there broad classes or approaches towards congestion control that can be identified? Which approaches have been adopted in practice, and why? And among those many "flavors"/variations of TCP that you might have heard about—how do they differ and in what scenarios are they best used, and why? So many questions!

To make sense of this and to answer all of these questions (and more) would require not just a book, but a great book! And now fortunately, there is such a book—this book! The three authors of *TCP Congestion Control: A Systems Approach* are among the most knowledgeable congestion control researchers on the planet—Brakmo and Peterson's TCP Vegas protocol (you can learn more about that in section 5.1) pioneered the notion that endpoints could anticipate and avoid congestion, rather than react to observed congestion; TCP Vegas has served as a foundation on which more recent congestion avoidance protocols (such as the BBR protocol championed by Google, see Section 5.3) have been designed. The authors are also absolutely fabulous writers (and I say this as a textbook author myself)—lucid, clear, and engaging, and able to organize and communicate complex ideas, with just the right amount of detail and discussion of practice. The "systems approach" that Larry Peterson and Bruce Davie have championed is also exactly what is needed to truly understand congestion control, where deep, system-wide issues in network architecture come to the fore (e.g., the separation and interaction of network and transport layer functionalities; the question of implementing networks services, such as congestion control, in the either the application layer or in the network).

This book is a needed and most welcome addition to the fabulous set of open source, "systems approach" books that Larry, Bruce and others have been developing. I hope you read it cover-to-cover, consult it again later as you need it in the future, and enjoy it as much as I have.

Jim Kurose
Amherst, Massachusetts

Preface

Congestion control has been one of the most active areas of research in computer networking from the earliest days of packet switching. The work of Jacobson and Karels in the 1980s laid the foundation for decades of subsequent work by introducing a suite of congestion control mechanisms into TCP. This was done at a time of crisis, with the Internet showing signs of congestion collapse. Ethernet inventor Bob Metcalf famously predicted the Internet would collapse in the 1990s and followed up on his promise to eat his words when it did not. But it was clear even then that congestion control was not a fully solved problem, and improvements to the algorithms on which the Internet's smooth functioning depends have multiplied ever since.

This book grew out of our own involvement in developing congestion control algorithms over the last three decades. There have been so many developments in congestion control over that time that it's nearly impossible to include all of them. What we have tried to do in this book is provide a framework for understanding congestion control as a systems problem, and to characterize the many approaches along a few main themes. For example, our work on TCP Vegas opened up a line of research that continues today, where the aim is to avoid severe congestion rather than react after it has set in. We thus consider avoidance-based approaches as one of the main categories of congestion control.

We expect this to be an evolving manuscript. There are many efforts in congestion control that are not currently covered, the algorithms that are covered continue to be refined, and new approaches will likely emerge to address new use cases. We will update the book as necessary to reflect the state of the field. Please help by submitting your comments and feedback. We also welcome contributions to the on-line annotated bibliography.

Finally, we extend our thanks to those who have contributed to the open source effort to improve this book. They include:

- Bill Fisher

- Giulio Micheloni

- J van Bemmel

- Omer Shapira

- Nico Vibert

- Vik Vanderlinden

Larry Peterson, Lawrence Brakmo, and Bruce Davie
May 2022

Chapter 1: Introduction

The Internet is considered an engineering success with few peers, and rightfully so. It has scaled to connect billions of devices, supports every imagined communications application, and accommodates transmission rates ranging from tens of bits per day to hundreds of gigabits per second. But at its core is a thorny technical challenge that has drawn widespread attention for the last 30-plus years, from both practitioners trying to make the Internet perform better and theoreticians wanting to understand its mathematical underpinnings: how the Internet's resources are best allocated to all the competing interests trying to use it.

Resource allocation is a hard problem in any computer system, but especially so for a system as complex as the Internet. The problem was not top-of-mind when the Internet's TCP/IP protocol stack was first deployed in the early 1980s. By the end of the decade, however, with the Internet gaining serious use in universities (but predating the World Wide Web's invention by several years), the network began to experience a phenomenon known as *congestion collapse*. A solution—congestion control—was developed and deployed in the late 1980s and the immediate crisis was addressed. The Internet community has been studying and refining its approach to congestion control ever since. This book is about that journey.

The most famous early efforts to manage congestion were undertaken by two researchers, Van Jacobson and Mike Karels. The resulting paper, *Congestion Avoidance and Control*, published in 1988, is one of the most cited papers in networking of all time. There are good reasons for that. One is that congestion collapse really did threaten the nascent Internet, and the work undertaken to address it was foundational to the Internet's ultimate success. Without that work it's unlikely we'd have the global Internet we have today.

Another reason for the citation impact of this work is that congestion control has been an amazingly fruitful area of research for over three decades. Congestion control, and resource allocation more broadly, are wide open design spaces with plenty of room for innovation. Decades of research and implementation have built on the early foundations, and it seems fair to assume that new approaches or refinements to the existing approaches will continue to appear for as long as the Internet exists.

In this book, we explore the design space for congestion control in the Internet and present a description of the major approaches to managing or avoiding congestion that have been developed over the last three decades.

Further Reading:
V. Jacobson. Congestion Avoidance and Control. ACM SIGCOMM '88 Symposium, August 1988.

1.1 What is Congestion?

Anyone who has driven on a highway at rush hour has experienced congestion. There is a limited resource—the space on the highway—and a set of cars, trucks, etc. that compete for that resource. As rush hour gets underway, more traffic arrives but the road keeps working as intended, just with more vehicles on it. But there comes a point where the number of vehicles becomes so large that everyone has to slow down (because there is no longer enough space for everyone to keep a safe distance at the speed limit) at which point the road actually becomes *less effective* at moving vehicles. So, just at the point when you would be wanting more capacity, there is actually less capacity to move traffic, as illustrated in Figure 1. This is the essence of *congestion collapse*, when congestion is so bad that the system starts to perform significantly worse than it did without congestion. The mechanism of congestion collapse is quite a bit different for packet networks than for highways, but it is equally problematic.[1]

This book focuses on congestion control for packet-switched networks. A fundamental aspect of packet switching is *multiplexing*, which is the means by which a system resource—such as a link or a

[1] Networking people like making analogies between real-world congestion and network congestion, but it's important to recognize that analogies are imperfect.

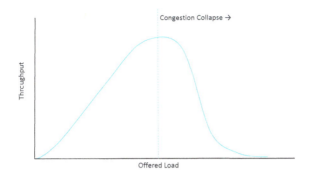

Figure 1: As load increases, throughput rises then falls at the point of congestion collapse.

queue in a router—is shared among multiple users or applications. In the case of the Internet, packet networks are *statistically multiplexed*, which means that, as packets show up somewhat randomly, we rely on the statistical properties of those arrivals to ensure that we don't run out of resources. The existence of congestion collapse shows that sometimes the statistics don't quite work out as we'd like.

To see how this might work, consider the simple network illustrated in Figure 2, where the three hosts on the left side of the network (senders S1-S3) are sending data to the three hosts on the right (receivers R1-R3) by sharing a switched network that contains only one physical link. (For simplicity, assume that host S1 is sending data to host R1, and so on.) In this situation, three flows of data—corresponding to the three pairs of hosts—are multiplexed onto a single physical link by switch 1 and then *demultiplexed* back into separate flows by switch 2. Note that we are being intentionally vague about exactly what a "flow of data" corresponds to for now, but we will make this more precise in later chapters.

Statistical multiplexing means that all the hosts in this network send packets whenever it suits them, and if it happens that several packets turn up at the same time at a switch, one of them will be transmitted first while the others are placed into a queue. So both the link and the queue are shared resources, and both are finite. The link can only carry so many bits per second, and the queue can only hold so many packets (or bytes) before it has to start discarding packets. Managing the access to these shared resources, and trying to do so in

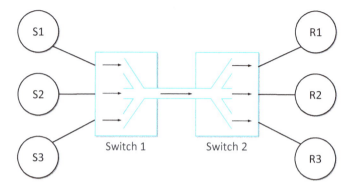

Figure 2: Multiplexing multiple logical flows over a single physical link.

a way that prevents congestion collapse, is the essence of congestion control. A switch that occasionally puts packets in a queue is operating normally. A switch that has large numbers of packets in its queues all or most of the time is congested. We'll get to the definition of congestion collapse for networks later on, but it starts with congested switches, routers or links.

For a deeper introduction to statistical multiplexing, and why it's the approach of choice for packet networks, we refer to our companion textbook.

When a switch builds a queue of packets awaiting transmission, it needs to decide which packet gets sent next. Each switch in a packet-switched network makes this decision independently, on a packet-by-packet basis. One of the issues that arises is how to make this decision in a fair manner. For example, many switches are designed to service packets on a first-in, first-out (FIFO) basis. Another approach would be to transmit the packets from each of the different flows that are currently sending data through the switch in a round-robin manner. This might be done to ensure that certain flows receive a particular share of the link's bandwidth or that they never have their packets delayed in the switch for more than a certain length of time. A network that attempts to allocate bandwidth to particular flows is sometimes said to support *Quality-of-Service (QoS)*.

One thing to take away from this discussion is that it is in the nature of packet-switched networks that they will sometimes be congested. The focus of this book is on the large body of work that has

Further Reading:
Requirements. *Computer Networks: A Systems Approach*, 2020.

been done to mitigate congestion, either by responding to it in effective ways to lessen it, or by preventing it before it occurs.

1.2 Controlling Congestion

Resource allocation and congestion control are complex issues that have been the subject of much study ever since the first network was designed. They are still active areas of research. One factor that makes these issues complex is that they are not isolated to a single level of a protocol hierarchy. Resource allocation is partially implemented in the routers, switches, and links inside the network and partially in the transport protocol running on the end hosts. End systems may use signalling protocols to convey their resource requirements to network nodes, which respond with information about resource availability. Application protocols may themselves be designed to mitigate congestion, for example, by changing the resolution of video transmission based on the current network conditions. This is a canonical example of a *systems issue*: you can't fully understand congestion without looking at all the places in the system that it touches.

We should clarify our terminology before going any further. By *resource allocation*, we mean the process by which network elements try to meet the competing demands that applications have for network resources—primarily link bandwidth and buffer space in routers or switches. Of course, it will often not be possible to meet all the demands, meaning that some users or applications may receive fewer network resources than they want. Part of the resource allocation problem is deciding when to say no and to whom.

We use the term *congestion control* to describe the efforts made by network nodes (including end systems) to prevent or respond to overload conditions. Since congestion is generally bad for everyone, the first order of business is making congestion subside, or preventing it in the first place. This might be achieved simply by persuading a few hosts to stop sending, thus improving the situation for everyone else. However, it is more common for congestion-control mechanisms to have some aspect of fairness—that is, they try to share the pain among all users, rather than causing great pain to a few. Thus, we see that many congestion-control mechanisms have some sort of resource allocation built into them.

It is also important to understand the difference between flow control and congestion control. Flow control involves keeping a fast sender from overrunning a slow receiver. Congestion control, by contrast, is intended to keep a set of senders from sending too much data *into the network* because of lack of resources at some point. These two concepts are often confused; as we will see, they also share some mechanisms.

Given all the different places and layers where congestion control and resource allocation can be implemented, it is helpful to start with a simple approach, which is what Jacobson and Karels did (although their solution ended up having quite a few moving parts).

In the early Internet, routers implemented the most basic resource allocation approach possible: FIFO queuing with tail drop. There was no awareness of flows or applications, so they simply accepted packets as they arrived, placed them in a queue whenever the outbound link capacity was less than the arrival rate, served the queue by the FIFO discipline, and dropped arriving packets if the queue was full ("tail-drop"). This is still the most common form of queuing today; we will discuss other approaches to queuing including *Active Queue Management* in a later chapter.

The reason that congestion collapse occurred in the early Internet is that dropped packets are not just discarded and forgotten. When the end-to-end transport protocol is TCP, as it is for most Internet traffic, a dropped packet will be retransmitted. So as congestion rises, the number of retransmitted packets rises; in other words, the number of packets sent into the network increases even if there is no real increase in the offered load from users and applications. More packets lead to more drops leading to more retransmissions and so on. You can see how this leads to collapse.

A useful term in this context is *goodput*, which is distinguished from throughput in the sense that only packets doing useful work are counted towards goodput. So, for example, if a link is running at 100% utilization, but 60% of the packets on that link are retransmitted due to earlier losses, you could say the goodput was only 40%.

The key insight of early researchers on congestion control was that it was possible and necessary for TCP to do something other than blindly retransmit lost packets during times of congestion. TCP would have to detect the congestion—which it can do, for example, by noticing the loss of packets—and then respond to the congestion by *reducing* the amount of traffic sent into the network. This interaction between the end-to-end protocol and the network during times of congestion formed the basis for much of today's congestion control and avoidance approaches. We'll get into the specifics of how these approaches work in subsequent chapters.

1.3 Theoretical Underpinnings

There has been a lot of important theoretical work done to understand congestion. At the core of congestion is queuing, and there is a huge body of theory behind queuing, much of which extends into other physical realms such as supermarket checkouts and road congestion. The standard reference on queuing for packet networks was written by one of the early pioneers of the ARPANET, Leonard Kleinrock.

Further Reading:
L. Kleinrock. Queueing Systems, Volume 2.

As packet networks became more widespread in the 1980s, there was a great deal of interest in how traffic behaved, with a growing realization that it might be more complex than had first been thought. One of the most popular models for data traffic was the Poisson model, which had worked well for various systems like call arrivals in the telephone network and people arriving at a queue in a supermarket. But the more that people studied the Internet and other packet networks, the worse the Poisson model started to look. There are a number of seminal papers that make the case for more complex models, of which the following are two.

These papers and others contributed to the consensus that Internet traffic is much more "bursty"—packets arrive in clumps—than had been assumed by early models. Furthermore, this burstiness displays *self-similarity*—a property of fractals, whereby when you zoom in, you keep seeing similar complexity at finer resolutions. For Internet traffic, this means that at any time scale, from microseconds to hours, you will see similar sorts of patterns.

Further Reading:
V. Paxson and S. Floyd. Wide-Area Traffic: The Failure of Poisson Modeling. IEEE/ACM Transactions on Networking, June 1995.

W. Leland *et al*, On the self-similar nature of Ethernet traffic. ACM SIGCOMM '93 Symposium, August 1993.

This research had a number of practical consequences, such as the realization that packet queues might get to be very long indeed, and thus routers and switches should have reasonably large packet buffers. (Correctly sizing those buffers became its own research topic.) Link utilizations could not be reliably kept close to 100% all the time, because you had to allow room for unpredictable bursts.

Two topics of particular importance when thinking about congestion avoidance are *fairness* and *stability*. When the network is congested, it's going to be necessary for some users or flows to send less. It is clearly worth asking: which flows should send less? Should all flows share the pain equally? And what happens if some flows pay more attention to congestion signals than others? These questions are at the heart of the fairness issue. Jain's *fairness index* is one of the widely accepted ways to measure how fair a network is. We dig into this topic in Chapter 3.

Stability is a critical property for any sort of control system, which is what congestion control is. Congestion is detected, some action is taken to reduce the total amount of traffic, causing congestion to ease, at which point it would seem reasonable to start sending more traffic again, leading back to more congestion. You can imagine that this sort of oscillation between congested and uncongested states could go on forever, and would be quite detrimental if the network is swinging from underutilized to collapsing. We really want it to find an equilibrium where the network is busy but not so much so that congestion collapse occurs. Finding these stable control loops has been one of the key challenges for congestion control system designers over the decades. The quest for stability features heavily in the early work of Jacobson and Karels and stability remains a requirement that subsequent approaches have to meet.

Once the initial congestion control algorithms of TCP were implemented and deployed, researchers began to build mathematical models of TCP's behavior. This enabled the relationship between packet loss rate, round-trip time, and throughput to be established. The foundation was laid in the paper by Mathis and colleagues, but there has been a body of work that is ongoing as the congestion control algorithms evolve. The idea that TCP would converge to a certain

throughput given stable conditions of RTT and loss also formed the
basis for *TCP-friendly rate control (TFRC)*. TFRC extends TCP-like congestion control to applications that don't use TCP, based on the idea
that they can still share available capacity in a fair way with those that
do. We return to this topic in Chapter 7.

Finally, much of the theoretical work on congestion control has
framed the problem as *"a distributed algorithm to share network resources
among competing sources, where the goal is to choose source rate so as to
maximize aggregate source utility subject to capacity constraints."* Formu-
lating a congestion-control mechanism as an algorithm to optimize
an objective function is traceable to a paper by Frank Kelly in 1997,
and later extended by Sanjeewa Athuraliya and Steven Low to take
into account both traffic sources (TCP) and router queuing techniques
(AQM).

This book does not pursue the mathematical formulation outlined
in these papers (and the large body of work that followed), but we
do find it helpful to recognize that there is an established connection
between optimizing a utility function and the pragmatic aspects of
the mechanisms described in this book. Congestion control is an area
of networking in which theory and practice have been productively
linked to explore the solution space and develop robust approaches to
the problem.

1.4 Congestion Control Today

It sometimes feels like networking protocols have all been nailed
down and standardized for decades, but few areas have remained
as dynamic as congestion control. While the early work by Jacobson,
Karels and others laid the foundation, there has been a long series
of innovations that continue today. We cover many of these in detail
in subsequent chapters, but you can rest assured that new ideas in
congestion control will continue to emerge for years to come.

Sometimes innovations are necessitated by changes in the landscape. For example, as bandwidths increased from megabits to gigabits per second, the amount of data in flight at any instant increased,
which raises the stakes for detecting and responding to congestion

Further Reading:
M. Mathis, J. Semke, J. Mah-
davi, and T. Ott. The Macro-
scopic Behavior of the TCP
Congestion Avoidance Algorithm. SIGCOMM CCR, 27(3),
July 1997.

Further Reading:
F. Kelly. Charging and Rate
Control for Elastic Traffic.
European Transactions on
Telecommunications, 8:33–37,
1997.

S. Athuraliya and S. Low,
An Empirical Validation of
a Duality Model of TCP and
Active Queue Management
Algorithms. Proceedings of the
Winter Simulation Conference,
2001.

quickly. High latency links, such as trans-oceanic cables and satellite links added to this problem by raising the round-trip time (RTT). These situations led to such innovations as using delay (and changes to delay) as a congestion signal (first seen in TCP Vegas). Also, with these "fatter pipes", there is a greater incentive to get the pipe filled quickly; you don't want to spend 10 RTTs figuring out how quickly you can send data if your message could have been sent in one or two RTTs. This led to efforts to more quickly determine the bottleneck bandwidth, such as XCP, RCP, and Quick-start for TCP.

Wireless networks, which became mainstream long after the early days of TCP, added a new issue to the mix: packet loss was no longer a reliable congestion signal, but could instead be attributed to a noisy radio channel. This led to a range of approaches to either hide the loss from the TCP hosts or to improve the mechanisms by which TCP detects congestion.

Cloud datacenters became another "use case" for congestion-control mechanisms. Unlike the Internet in general, where end-to-end latencies are highly variable, the RTT in a datacenter is both predictable and relatively small (<10ms). And because the network is highly regular in structure (e.g., a leaf-spine fabric), it is well-understood where and under what circumstances congestion is likely to occur. This makes TCP running in a datacenter ripe for a purpose-tuned algorithm rather than having to use the general-purpose mechanism that runs on the global Internet.

New applications have also contributed to the interest in improving congestion control. One salient example is the rise of video streaming as the (currently) dominant source of traffic on the Internet. Again, there were many approaches developed to make video work better under conditions of congestion. One that has enjoyed great success is *Dynamic Adaptive Streaming over HTTP (DASH)*, in which the server delivering the video switches from one quality of encoding to another (and hence from one bit-rate to another) in response to the measured congestion on the path to the receiver. This moves the congestion control loop up to the application layer, or rather, it adds a second control loop on top of the one already provided by TCP.

This quick tour of innovations is hardly exhaustive, and we will see more detail on these and other approaches in the coming chapters. The important thing to understand at this point is that congestion control continues to evolve as the technology landscape and application requirements change.

1.5 Reference Implementation

We saw in Section 1.3 that there is a rich body of literature studying the mathematical properties of congestion-control algorithms, yet congestion control remains a highly pragmatic concern. It is estimated that TCP connections carry 85% of the traffic on the Internet, and those connections are anchored in software implementations of TCP running in every imaginable OS (e.g., Linux, Windows, MacOS, iOS, Android). As a practical matter, the very specification of the congestion-control mechanisms we discuss in this book is represented in kernel-level code, typically implemented in C. The theory defines abstract models of this code, but the code *specifies* the algorithm.

If the implementation is effectively the specification, then which implementation is authoritative; which is the *reference implementation?* The answer has been the dominant open source implementation of the day. This was originally the *Berkeley Software Distribution (BSD)* implementation of Unix, and in fact, the initial algorithm proposed by Jacobson and Karels was a noteworthy feature of the Tahoe release of BSD 4.3 in 1988. This connection between BSD Unix and the TCP congestion-control algorithms was so strong that the variants of algorithm became known (named) according to the BSD release: e.g., TCP Tahoe, and later TCP Reno.

BSD and its descendants continue to this day (notably as FreeBSD), but it was eventually overtaken by Linux, in the early 2000s, as the *de facto* open source, Unix-based OS. All the variants of TCP congestion control described in this book are available (and can be optionally activated) in the Linux kernel. They have become the reference implementation of those algorithms, which leads us to our final point: The standard for evaluating TCP congestion-control mechanisms is empirical, by running real traffic between Linux-based implementations

Further Reading:
S.J. Leffler, M.K. McKusick, M.J. Karels, and J.S Quarterman. The Design and Implementation of the 4.3 BSD UNIX Operating System. Addison-Wesley. January 1989.

of TCP senders and receivers. The open question is: What traffic, and over what network?

Berkeley Unix

Any student of the Internet should have an appreciation for the role Berkeley Unix (aka BSD) played in the success of the Internet. Unix, of course, originated at AT&T Bell Labs in the early 1970s, but it was an investment by DARPA to support an open source implementation of Unix—which was to include the fledgling TCP/IP protocol stack—that proved to be transformative.

At the time, the success of the Internet was not a foregone conclusion. It was viewed by many as a research curiosity, and certainly did not enjoy much support within the computing and telecommunication incumbents of the day. It was largely because universities (and their students) had access to an open implementation of the Internet protocol stack, and affordable hardware to run it on, that TCP/IP took root. Seeding transformative technology through open source software and readily available hardware has proven to be a powerful strategy, of which BSD is an early success story.

While useful insights can often be gained by observing the behavior of TCP connections running across the actual Internet, the wide variability (in both time and space) of "the Internet" makes controlled experiments virtually impossible. Instead, the current best-practice is to run a collection of "representative flows" over isolated but "representative network topologies." There is no established gold standard for either the set of flows or the set of network topologies, so experimental results are never definitive. But the body of evidence collected using this methodology has proven sufficient to advance the state-of-the-art over the years.

For the purposes of this book, we use the experimental methodology described in Chapter 3. We use it to both visualize the behavior of the various algorithms (helping to build intuition) and to highlight problematic scenarios that continue to make congestion control such a challenging and interesting technical problem.

Chapter 2: Background

To understand the Internet's approach to congestion, it's necessary to first talk about the assumptions and design decisions built into the Internet architecture. This chapter does that, and in doing so, gives enough detail about the TCP/IP protocol stack to understand the specifics of the congestion control mechanisms introduced in later chapters. For more complete coverage of TCP and IP, we recommend our companion textbook.

Further Reading:
Computer Networks: A Systems Approach, 2020.

2.1 Best-Effort Packet Delivery

The Internet supports a *connectionless, best-effort* packet delivery service model, as specified by the Internet Protocol (IP) and implemented by switches and routers. Being *connectionless* means every IP packet carries enough information for the network to forward it to its correct destination; there is no setup mechanism to tell the network what to do when packets arrive. *Best-effort* means that if something goes wrong and the packet gets lost, corrupted, or misdelivered while en route, the network does nothing to recover from the failure; recovering from such errors is the responsibility of higher level protocols running on end hosts. This approach was intentionally designed to keep routers as simple as possible, and is generally viewed as consistent with the *end-to-end argument* articulated by Saltzer, Reed, and Clark.

One consequence of this design is that a given source may have ample capacity to send traffic into the network at some rate, but somewhere in the middle of the network its packets encounter a bottleneck link that is being used by many different traffic sources. Figure 3 il-

Further Reading:
J. Saltzer, D. Reed, and D. Clark. End-to-End Arguments in System Design. ACM Transactions on Computer Systems, Nov. 1984.

lustrates an acute example of this situation—two high-speed links are leading into a router which then feeds outgoing traffic onto a low-speed link. The router is able to queue (buffer) packets for a while, but if the problem persists, the queue will first grow to some length, and eventually (because it is finite) it will overflow, leading to packet loss. This situation, where offered load exceeds link capacity, is the very definition of congestion.

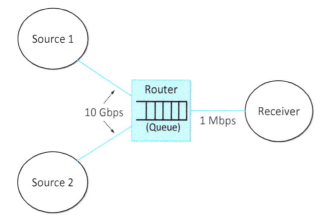

Note that avoiding congestion is not a problem that can be fully addressed by routing. While it is true that a congested link could be assigned a large "cost" by a routing protocol, in an effort to make traffic avoid that link, this can't solve the overall problem of too much traffic being offered to a bottleneck link. To see this, we need look no further than the simple network depicted in Figure 3, where all traffic has to flow through the same router to reach the destination. Although this is an extreme example, it is common to have at least one link that it is not possible to route around. This link, and the router that feeds packets into it, can become congested, and there is nothing the routing mechanism can do about it.

2.1.1 Flows and Soft State

Because the Internet assumes a connectionless model, any connection-oriented service is implemented by an end-to-end transport protocol running on the end hosts (such as TCP). There is no connection setup phase implemented within the network (in contrast to virtual circuit based networks), and as a consequence, there is no mechanism for individual routers to pre-allocate buffer space or link bandwidth to active connections.

The lack of an explicit connection setup phase does not imply that routers must be completely unaware of end-to-end connections. IP packets are switched independently, but it is often the case that a given pair of hosts exchange many packets consecutively, e.g. as a large video file is downloaded by a client from a server. Furthermore, a given stream of packets between a pair of hosts often flows through a consistent set of routers. This idea of a *flow*—a sequence of packets sent between a source/destination pair and following the same route through the network—is an important abstraction that we will use in later chapters.

One of the powers of the flow abstraction is that flows can be defined at different granularities. For example, a flow can be host-to-host (i.e., have the same source/destination IP addresses) or process-to-process (i.e., have the same source/destination host/port pairs). Figure 4 illustrates several flows passing through a series of routers.

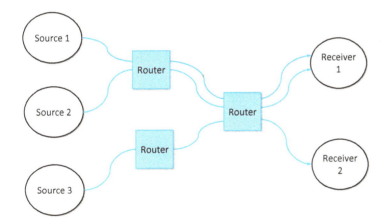

Figure 4: Multiple flows passing through a set of routers.

Because multiple related packets flow through each router, it sometimes makes sense to maintain some state information for each flow, which can be used to make resource allocation decisions about the packets of that flow. This is called *soft state*, where the main difference between soft and hard state is that the former is not explicitly created and removed by signalling. Soft state represents a middle ground between a purely connectionless network that maintains *no* state at the routers and a purely connection-oriented network that maintains hard state at the routers. In general, the correct operation of the network does not depend on soft state being present (each packet is still routed correctly without regard to this state), but when a packet happens to belong to a flow for which the router is currently maintaining soft state, then the router is better able to handle the packet.

Quality-of-Service

With best-effort service, all packets are given essentially equal treatment, with end hosts given no opportunity to ask the network that some packets or flows be given certain guarantees or preferential service. Defining a service model that supports some kind of preferred service or guarantee—for example, guaranteeing the bandwidth needed for a video stream—results in an architecture that supports multiple qualities of service (QoS).

There is actually a spectrum of possibilities, ranging from a purely best-effort service model to one in which individual flows receive quantitative guarantees of QoS. There are extensions to the Internet's service model that includes additional levels of service, but (1) they are not widely deployed throughout the Internet, and (2) even when they are deployed, they still allow for best-effort traffic, which operates according to the congestion control algorithms described in the book.

2.1.2 IP Packet Format

For completeness, Figure 5 gives the IPv4 packet format, but it is the 8-bit TOS (Type of Service) field that is relevant to our discussion. This field has been interpreted in different ways over the years, but its basic function is to allow packets to be treated differently based on application needs. In later chapters we will see how various congestion control mechanisms have applied different meanings to the TOS field over time.

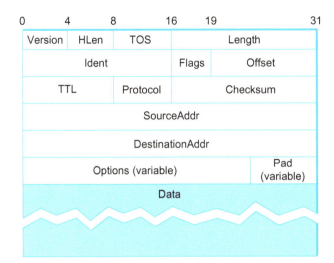

Figure 5: IPv4 packet header.

2.1.3 FIFO Queuing

Each router implements some queuing discipline that governs how packets are buffered while waiting to be transmitted. The queuing algorithm can be thought of as allocating both bandwidth (which packets get transmitted) and buffer space (which packets get discarded). It also directly affects the latency experienced by a packet by determining how long a packet waits to be transmitted.

The most common queuing algorithm is *First-In/First-Out (FIFO)*, where the first packet that arrives at a router is the first packet to be transmitted. This is illustrated in Figure 6(a), which shows a FIFO queue with "slots" to hold up to eight packets. Packets are added at the tail as they arrive, and transmitted from the head. Thus, FIFO ordering is preserved.

Given that the amount of buffer space at each router is finite, if a packet arrives and the queue (buffer space) is full, then the router discards that packet, as shown in Figure 6(b). This is done without regard to which flow the packet belongs to or how important the packet is. This is sometimes called *tail drop*, since packets that arrive at the tail end of the FIFO are dropped if the queue is full.

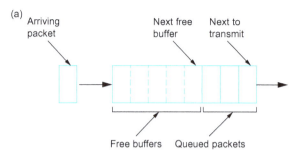

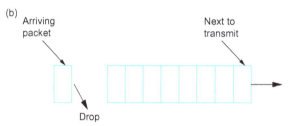

Figure 6: FIFO queuing (a), and tail drop at a FIFO queue (b).

Note that tail drop and FIFO are two separable ideas. FIFO is a *scheduling discipline*—it determines the order in which packets are transmitted. Tail drop is a *drop policy*—it determines which packets get dropped. Because FIFO and tail drop are the simplest instances of scheduling discipline and drop policy, respectively, they are sometimes viewed as a bundle—the default queuing implementation. Chapter 6 examines other drop policies, which use a more complex algorithm than "Is there a free buffer?" to decide when to drop packets. Such a drop policy may be used with FIFO, or with more complex scheduling disciplines.

Fair Queuing

Fair Queuing (FQ) is an alternative to FIFO queuing, commonly used to implement QoS guarantees. The idea of FQ is to maintain a separate queue for each flow currently being handled by the router (for some flow granularity). The router then services these queues in round-robin order (in the simplest version of FQ). If the router is congested with traffic from several flows, FQ ensures that no single flow can dominate the outgoing link—each flow will get a share of the link. In this way, a given source cannot arbitrarily increase its share of the network's capacity at the expense of other flows.

FQ can be used in conjunction with an end-to-end congestion-control mechanism. It simply segregates traffic so that ill-behaved traffic sources do not interfere with those that are faithfully implementing the end-to-end algorithm. FQ also enforces fairness among a collection of flows managed by a well-behaved congestion-control algorithm.

2.2 Reliable Byte-Stream

TCP implements a reliable byte stream—between a pair of processes running on end hosts—on top of the best-effort service model supported by IP. This section describes TCP in sufficient detail to understand the congestion control mechanisms described in later chapters.

2.2.1 End-to-End Issues

At the heart of TCP is the sliding window algorithm, which in addition to its familiar acknowledgment/timeout/retransmit mechanism, has to address the following complications.

First, because TCP supports logical connections between two processes that are running on any two computers connected to the Internet, it needs an explicit connection establishment phase during which the two sides agree to exchange data with each other. One of the things that happens during connection establishment is that the two parties establish some shared state to enable the sliding window algorithm to begin. Connection teardown is needed so each host knows it is OK to free this state.

Second, TCP connections are likely to have widely different round-trip times. For example, a TCP connection between San Francisco and Boston, which are separated by several thousand kilometers, might have an RTT of 100 ms, while a TCP connection between two hosts in the same room might have an RTT of only 1 ms. The same TCP protocol must be able to support both of these connections. To make matters worse, the TCP connection between San Francisco and

Boston might have an RTT of 100 ms at 3 a.m., but an RTT of 500 ms at 3 p.m. Variations in the RTT are even possible during a single TCP connection that lasts only a few minutes. What this means to the sliding window algorithm is that the timeout mechanism that triggers retransmissions must be adaptive.

Third, due to the best-effort nature of the Internet, packets may be reordered while in transit. Packets that are slightly out of order do not cause a problem since the sliding window algorithm can re-order packets correctly using the sequence number. The real issue is how far out of order packets can get or, said another way, how late a packet can arrive at the destination. In the worst case, a packet can be delayed in the Internet almost arbitrarily. Each time a packet is forwarded by a router, the IP time to live (TTL) field is decremented, and eventually it reaches zero, at which time the packet is discarded (and hence there is no danger of it arriving late). Note that TTL is something of a misnomer and was renamed to the more accurate Hop Count in IPv6. Knowing that IP throws packets away after their TTL expires, TCP assumes that each packet has a maximum lifetime. The exact lifetime, known as the *Maximum Segment Lifetime (MSL)*, is an engineering choice. The current recommended setting is 120 seconds. Keep in mind that IP does not directly enforce this 120-second value; it is simply a conservative estimate that TCP makes of how long a packet might live in the Internet. The implication is significant—TCP has to be prepared for very old packets to suddenly show up at the receiver, potentially confusing the sliding window algorithm.

Fourth, because almost any kind of computer can be connected to the Internet, the amount of resources dedicated to any given TCP connection is highly variable, especially considering that any one host can potentially support hundreds of TCP connections at the same time. This means that TCP must include a mechanism that each side uses to "learn" what resources (e.g., how much buffer space) the other side is able to apply to the connection. This is the flow control issue.

Fifth, the sending side of a TCP connection has no idea what links will be traversed to reach the destination. For example, the sending machine might be directly connected to a relatively fast Ethernet—and capable of sending data at a rate of 10 Gbps—but somewhere out in the middle of the network, a 1.5 Mbps link must be traversed. And, to make matters worse, data being generated by many different sources might be trying to traverse this same slow link. Even a fast link will get congested if enough flows converge on it. This is the essential factor leading to congestion, which we will address in later chapters.

2.2.2 *Segment Format*

TCP is a byte-oriented protocol, which means that the sender writes bytes into a TCP connection and the receiver reads bytes out of the TCP connection. Although "byte stream" describes the service TCP offers to application processes, TCP does not, itself, transmit individual bytes over the Internet. Instead, TCP on the source host buffers enough bytes from the sending process to fill a reasonably sized packet and then sends this packet to its peer on the destination host. TCP on the destination host then empties the contents of the packet into a receive buffer, and the receiving process reads from this buffer at its leisure. This situation is illustrated in Figure 7, which, for simplicity, shows data flowing in only one direction.

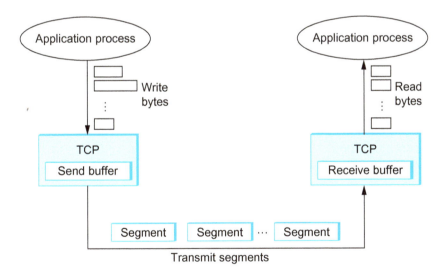

Figure 7: How TCP manages a byte stream.

The packets exchanged between TCP peers in Figure 7 are called *segments*, since each one carries a segment of the byte stream. Each

TCP segment contains the header schematically depicted in Figure 8. The following introduces the fields that will be relevant to our discussion.

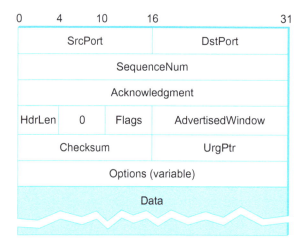

Figure 8: TCP header format.

The SrcPort and DstPort fields identify the source and destination ports, respectively. These two fields, plus the source and destination IP addresses, combine to uniquely identify each TCP connection. All state needed to manage a TCP connection, including the congestion-related state introduced in later chapters, is bound to the 4-tuple: (SrcPort, SrcIPAddr, DstPort, DstIPAddr).

The Acknowledgment, SequenceNum, and AdvertisedWindow fields are all involved in TCP's sliding window algorithm. Because TCP is a byte-oriented protocol, each byte of data has a sequence number. The SequenceNum field contains the sequence number for the first byte of data carried in that segment, and the Acknowledgment and Advertised-Window fields carry information about the flow of data going in the other direction. To simplify our discussion, we ignore the fact that data can flow in both directions, and we concentrate on data that has a particular SequenceNum flowing in one direction and Acknowledg-ment and AdvertisedWindow values flowing in the opposite direction, as illustrated in Figure 9.

The 6-bit Flags field is used to relay control information between TCP peers. They include the SYN and FIN flags, which are used when

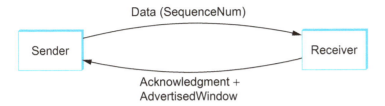

Figure 9: Simplified illustration (showing only one direction) of the TCP process, with data flow in one direction and ACKs in the other.

establishing and terminating a connection, and the ACK flag, which is set any time the Acknowledgment field is valid (implying that the receiver should pay attention to it).

Finally, the TCP header is of variable length (options can be attached after the mandatory fields), and so the HdrLen field is included to give the length of the header in 32-bit words. This field is relevant when TCP extensions are appended to the end of the header, for example, in support of congestion control. The significance of adding these extensions as options rather than changing the core of the TCP header is that hosts can still communicate using TCP even if they do not implement the options. Hosts that do implement the optional extensions, however, can take advantage of them. The two sides agree that they will use the options during TCP's connection establishment phase.

2.2.3 *Reliable and Ordered Delivery*

TCP's variant of the sliding window algorithm serves two main purposes: (1) it guarantees the reliable, in-order delivery of data, and (2) it enforces flow control between the sender and the receiver. To implement flow control, the receiver chooses a sliding window size and *advertises* it to the sender using the AdvertisedWindow field in the TCP header. The sender is then limited to having no more than a value of AdvertisedWindow bytes of unacknowledged data at any given time. The receiver selects a suitable value for AdvertisedWindow based on the amount of memory allocated to the connection for the purpose of buffering data. The idea is to keep the sender from over-running the receiver's buffer.

To see how TCP's sliding window works, consider the situation illustrated in Figure 10. TCP on the sending side maintains a send buffer. This buffer is used to store data that has been sent but not yet acknowledged, as well as data that has been written by the sending application but not transmitted. On the receiving side, TCP maintains a receive buffer. This buffer holds data that arrives out of order, as well as data that is in the correct order (i.e., there are no missing bytes earlier in the stream) but that the application process has not yet had the chance to read.

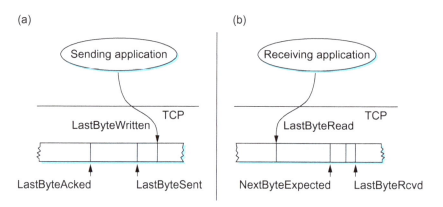

Figure 10: Relationship between TCP send buffer (a) and receive buffer (b).

To make the following discussion simpler to follow, we initially ignore the fact that both the buffers and the sequence numbers are of some finite size and hence will eventually wrap around. Also, we do not distinguish between a pointer into a buffer where a particular byte of data is stored and the sequence number for that byte.

Looking first at the sending side, three pointers are maintained into the send buffer, each with an obvious meaning: LastByteAcked, LastByteSent, and LastByteWritten. Clearly,

$$\text{LastByteAcked} \leq \text{LastByteSent} \leq \text{LastByteWritten}$$

since the receiver cannot have acknowledged a byte that has not yet been sent, and TCP cannot send a byte that the application process has not yet written.

A similar set of pointers (sequence numbers) are maintained on the receiving side: LastByteRead, NextByteExpected, and LastByteRcvd. The inequalities are a little less intuitive, however, because of the problem of out-of-order delivery. In this case:

$$\mathsf{LastByteRead} < \mathsf{NextByteExpected} \leq \mathsf{LastByteRcvd} + 1$$

since a byte cannot be read by the application until it is received *and* all preceding bytes have also been received. If data has arrived in order, NextByteExpected points to the byte after LastByteRcvd, whereas if data has arrived out of order, then NextByteExpected points to the start of the first gap in the data, as in Figure 10.

2.2.4 Flow Control

The discussion up to this point assumes the receiver is able to keep pace with the sender, but because this is not necessarily the case and the both the sender and receiver have buffers of some fixed size, the receiver needs some way to slow down the sender. This is the essence of flow control.

   While we have already pointed out that flow control and congestion control are different problems, it's important to understand how flow control works first, because the windowing mechanism used to implement flow control turns out to have an important role in congestion control too. Windowing provides the sender with clear instructions on how much data can be "in flight" (not yet acknowledged) which is essential for both problems.

   In what follows, we reintroduce the fact that both buffers are of some finite size, denoted SendBufferSize and RcvBufferSize, respectively. The receiver throttles the sender by advertising a window that is no larger than the amount of data that it can buffer. Observe that TCP on the receive side must keep

$$\mathsf{LastByteRcvd} - \mathsf{LastByteRead} \leq \mathsf{RcvBufferSize}$$

to avoid overflowing its buffer. It therefore advertises a window size of

$$\mathsf{AdvertisedWindow} = \mathsf{RcvBufferSize} - ((\mathsf{NextByteExpected} - 1) - \mathsf{LastByteRead})$$

which represents the amount of free space remaining in its buffer. As data arrives, the receiver acknowledges it as long as all the preceding bytes have also arrived. In addition, LastByteRcvd moves to the right (is incremented), meaning that the advertised window potentially shrinks. Whether or not it shrinks depends on how fast the local application process is consuming data. If the local process is reading data just as fast as it arrives (causing LastByteRead to be incremented at the same rate as LastByteRcvd), then the advertised window stays open (i.e., AdvertisedWindow = RcvBufferSize). If, however, the receiving process falls behind, perhaps because it performs a very expensive operation on each byte of data that it reads, then the advertised window grows smaller with every segment that arrives, until it eventually goes to 0.

TCP on the send side must then adhere to the advertised window it gets from the receiver. This means that at any given time, it must ensure that

$$\text{LastByteSent} - \text{LastByteAcked} \leq \text{AdvertisedWindow}$$

Said another way, the sender computes an *effective* window that limits how much data it can send:

$$\text{EffectiveWindow} = \text{AdvertisedWindow} - (\text{LastByteSent} - \text{LastByteAcked})$$

Clearly, EffectiveWindow must be greater than 0 before the source can send more data. It is possible, therefore, that a segment arrives acknowledging x bytes, thereby allowing the sender to increment LastByteAcked by x, but because the receiving process was not reading any data, the advertised window is now x bytes smaller than the time before. In such a situation, the sender would be able to free buffer space, but not to send any more data.

All the while this is going on, the send side must also make sure that the local application process does not overflow the send buffer—that is,

$$\text{LastByteWritten} - \text{LastByteAcked} \leq \text{SendBufferSize}$$

If the sending process tries to write b bytes to TCP, but

$$(\mathsf{LastByteWritten} - \mathsf{LastByteAcked}) + b > \mathsf{SendBufferSize}$$

then TCP blocks the sending process and does not allow it to generate more data.

It is now possible to understand how a slow receiving process ultimately stops a fast sending process. First, the receive buffer fills up, which means the advertised window shrinks to 0. An advertised window of 0 means that the sending side cannot transmit any data, even though the previously sent data has been successfully acknowledged. Finally, not being able to transmit any data means that the send buffer fills up, which ultimately causes TCP to block the sending process. As soon as the receiving process starts to read data again, the receive-side TCP is able to open its window back up, which allows the send-side TCP to transmit data out of its buffer. When this data is eventually acknowledged, LastByteAcked is incremented, the buffer space holding this acknowledged data becomes free, and the sending process is unblocked and allowed to proceed.

There is only one remaining detail that must be resolved—how does the sending side know that the advertised window is no longer 0? TCP *always* sends a segment in response to a received data segment, and this response contains the latest values for the Acknowledge and AdvertisedWindow fields, even if these values have not changed since the last time they were sent. The problem is this: Once the receive side has advertised a window size of 0, the sender is not permitted to send any more data, which means it has no way to discover that the advertised window is no longer 0 at some time in the future. TCP on the receive side does not spontaneously send non-data segments; it only sends them in response to an arriving data segment.

TCP deals with this situation as follows. Whenever the other side advertises a window size of 0, the sending side persists in sending a 1 byte segment every so often. It knows this data will probably not be accepted, but it tries anyway, because each of these segments triggers a response that contains the current advertised window, which will eventually be nonzero. These 1-byte messages are called *Zero Window Probes* and in practice they are sent every 5 to 60 seconds.

2.2.5 *Triggering Transmission*

We next consider the surprisingly subtle issue of how TCP decides to transmit a segment. If we ignore flow control and assume the window is wide open, then TCP has three mechanisms to trigger the transmission of a segment:

- TCP maintains a variable, typically called the *maximum segment size* (MSS), and it sends a segment as soon as it has collected MSS bytes from the sending process.

- The sending process explicitly asks TCP to send a segment by invoking a *push* operation. This causes TCP to flush the buffer of unsent bytes.

- A timer fires, resulting in a segment that contains as many bytes as are currently buffered for transmission.

Of course, we can't just ignore flow control. If the sender has MSS bytes of data to send and the window is open at least that much, then the sender transmits a full segment. Suppose, however, that the sender is accumulating bytes to send, but the window is currently closed. Now suppose an ACK arrives that effectively opens the window enough for the sender to transmit, say, MSS/2 bytes. Should the sender transmit a half-full segment or wait for the window to open to a full MSS?

The original specification was silent on this point, and early implementations of TCP decided to go ahead and transmit a half-full segment. But it turns out that the strategy of aggressively taking advantage of any available window led to a situation now known as the *silly window syndrome*, whereby partial segments could not be coalesced back into a full segment. This led to the introduction of a more sophisticated decision process known as Nagle's Algorithm, which we introduce here because it becomes a central part of the strategy adopted by the congestion-control mechanisms described in later chapters.

The central question Nagle answers is this: How long does the sender wait when the effective window is open less than MSS? If we wait too long, then we hurt interactive applications. If we don't wait long enough, then we risk sending a bunch of tiny packets and falling into the silly window syndrome.

While TCP could use a clock-based timer—for example, one that fires every 100 ms—Nagle introduced an elegant *self-clocking* solution. The idea is that as long as TCP has any data in flight, the sender will eventually receive an ACK. This ACK can be treated like a timer firing, triggering the transmission of more data. Nagle's algorithm provides a simple, unified rule for deciding when to transmit:

```
When the application produces data to send
    if both the available data and the window >= MSS
        send a full segment
    else
        if there is unACKed data in flight
            buffer the new data until an ACK arrives
        else
            send all the new data now
```

In other words, it's always OK to send a full segment if the window allows. It's also alright to immediately send a small amount of data if there are currently no segments in transit, but if there is anything in flight, the sender must wait for an ACK before transmitting the next segment. Thus, an interactive application that continually writes one byte at a time will send data at a rate of one segment per RTT. Some segments will contain a single byte, while others will contain as many bytes as the user was able to type in one round-trip time. Because some applications cannot afford such a delay for each write it does to a TCP connection, the socket interface allows the application to set the TCP_NODELAY option, meaning that data is transmitted as soon as possible.

2.3 High-Speed Networks

TCP was first deployed in the early 1980s, when backbone networks had link bandwidths measured in the tens of kilobits per second. It should not come as a surprise that significant attention has gone into adapting TCP for ever-increasing network speeds. In principle, the resulting changes are independent of the congestion control mechanisms presented in later chapters, but they were deployed in concert with those changes, which unfortunately, conflates the two issues. To further blur the line between accommodating high-speed networks and addressing congestion, there are extensions to the TCP header that play a dual role in addressing both. Finally, note that increasing bandwidth-delay product *does* have an impact on congestion control, and some of the approaches discussed in later chapters deal with that issue.

This section focuses on the challenges of high-speed networks, and we postpone the details about the TCP extensions used to address those challenges until Chapter 4, where we also take the related congestion control mechanisms into account. For now, we focus on limitations of the SequenceNum and AdvertisedWindow fields, and the implication they have on TCP's correctness and performance.

2.3.1 Protecting Against Wraparound

The relevance of the 32-bit sequence number space is that the sequence number used on a given connection might wrap around—a byte with sequence number S could be sent at one time, and then at a later time a second byte with the same sequence number S might be sent. Once again, we assume that packets cannot survive in the Internet for longer than the recommended MSL. Thus, we currently need to make sure that the sequence number does not wrap around within a 120-second period of time. Whether or not this happens depends on how fast data can be transmitted over the Internet—that is, how fast the 32-bit sequence number space can be consumed. (This discussion assumes that we are trying to consume the sequence number space as fast as possible, but of course we will be if we are doing our job of keeping the pipe full.) Table 1 shows how long it takes for the sequence number to wrap around on networks with various bandwidths.

The 32-bit sequence number space is adequate at modest bandwidths, but given that OC-192 links are now common in the Internet

Bandwidth	Time until Wraparound
T1 (1.5 Mbps)	6.2 hours
T3 (44.7 Mbps)	12.8 minutes
OC-3 (148.6 Mbps)	3.9 minutes
OC-48 (2.4 Gbps)	14.3 seconds
OC-192 (9.5 Gbps)	3.6 seconds
10GigE (10 Gbps)	3.4 seconds

Table 1: Time Until 32-Bit Sequence Number Space Wraps Around.

backbone, and that most servers now come with 10Gig Ethernet (or 10 Gbps) interfaces, we are now well-past the point where 32 bits is too small. A TCP extension doubles the size of the sequence number field to protect against the SequenceNum field wrapping. This extension plays a dual role in congestion control, so we postpone the details until Chapter 4.

2.3.2 *Keeping the Pipe Full*

The relevance of the 16-bit AdvertisedWindow field is that it must be big enough to allow the sender to keep the pipe full. Clearly, the receiver is free to not open the window as large as the AdvertisedWindow field allows; we are interested in the situation in which the receiver has enough buffer space to handle as much data as the largest possible AdvertisedWindow allows.

In this case, it is not just the network bandwidth but the bandwidth-delay product that dictates how big the AdvertisedWindow field needs to be—the window needs to be opened far enough to allow a full bandwidth-delay product's worth of data to be transmitted. Assuming an RTT of 100 ms (a typical number for a cross-country connection in the United States), Table 2 gives the bandwidth-delay product for several network technologies. Note that for the OC-n links we've used the available link bandwidth after removing SONET overhead.

In other words, TCP's AdvertisedWindow field is in even worse shape than its SequenceNum field—it is not big enough to handle even a T3 connection across the continental United States, since a 16-bit field allows us to advertise a window of only 64 KB.

The fix is an extension to TCP that allows the receiver to advertise

Bandwidth	Bandwidth × Delay Product
T1 (1.5 Mbps)	18.8 KB
T3 (44.7 Mbps)	546.1 KB
OC-3 (148.6 Mbps)	1.8 MB
OC-48 (2.4 Gbps)	28.7 MB
OC-192 (9.5 Gbps)	113.4 MB
10GigE (10 Gbps)	119.2 MB

Table 2: Required Window Size for 100-ms RTT

a larger window, thereby allowing the sender to fill larger bandwidth-delay product pipes that are made possible by high-speed networks. This extension involves an option that defines a *scaling factor* for the advertised window. That is, rather than interpreting the number that appears in the AdvertisedWindow field as indicating how many bytes the sender is allowed to have unacknowledged, this option allows the two sides of TCP to agree that the AdvertisedWindow field counts larger chunks (e.g., how many 16-byte units of data the sender can have un-acknowledged). In other words, the window scaling option specifies how many bits each side should left-shift the AdvertisedWindow field before using its contents to compute an effective window.

Chapter 3: Design Space

With the architectural foundation of TCP/IP in place, we are ready to explore the design space for addressing congestion. But to do this, it is helpful to first take a step back and consider the bigger picture. The Internet is a complex arrangement of compute, storage, and communication resources that is shared among millions of users. The challenge is how to assign those resources—specifically switching capacity, buffer space, and link bandwidth—to end-to-end packet flows.

Because the Internet originally adopted a best-effort service model, and users (or more precisely, TCP running on their behalf) were free to send as many packets into the network as they could generate, it was not surprising that the Internet eventually suffered from the *tragedy of the commons*. And with users starting to experience congestion collapse, the natural response was to try to control it. Hence the term *congestion control*, which can be viewed as an implicit mechanism for allocating resources. It is implicit in the sense that as the control mechanism detects resources becoming scarce, it reacts in an effort to alleviate congestion.

A network service model in which resources are *explicitly* allocated to packet flows is the obvious alternative; for example, an application could make an explicit request for resources before sending traffic. The best-effort assumption of IP meant such an approach was not immediately viable at the time congestion became a serious issue. Subsequent work was done to retrofit more explicit resource allocation mechanisms to the Internet's best-effort delivery model, including the ability to make *Quality-of-Service (QoS)* guarantees. It is instructive to consider the Internet's approach to congestion in the context of such efforts. The first section does so as it explores the set of design decisions that underlie the control mechanisms outlined in this book. We then define the criteria by which different congestion-control mechanisms can be quantitatively evaluated and compared.

3.1 Implementation Choices

We start by introducing four implementation choices that a congestion control mechanism faces, and the design rationale behind the decisions that were made for TCP/IP. Some of the decisions were "obvious" given the circumstances under which they were made, but for completeness—and because the Internet's continual evolution means circumstances change—it is prudent to consider them all.

3.1.1 Centralized versus Distributed

In principle, the first design decision is whether a network's approach to resource allocation is centralized or distributed. In practice, the Internet's scale—along with the autonomy of the organizations that connect to it—dictated a distributed approach. Indeed, distributed management of resources was an explicitly stated goal of the Internet's design, as articulated by Dave Clark. But acknowledging this default decision is important for two reasons.

Further Reading:
D. Clark, The Design Philosophy of the DARPA Internet Protocols. ACM SIGCOMM, 1988.

First, while the Internet's approach to congestion control is distributed across its millions of hosts and routers, it is fair to think of them as cooperatively trying to achieve a globally optimal solution. From this perspective, there is a shared objective function, and all the elements are implementing a distributed algorithm to optimize that function. The various mechanisms described throughout this book are simply defining different objective functions, where a persistent challenge has been how to think about competing objective functions when multiple mechanisms have been deployed.

Second, while a centralized approach is not practical for the Internet as a whole, it can be appropriate for limited domains. For example, a logically centralized controller could collect information about the state of the network's links and switches, compute a globally optimal allocation, and then advise (or even police) end hosts as to how much capacity is available to each of them. Such an approach would certainly be limited by the time-scale in which the centralized controller could be responsive to changes in the network, but it has been successfully applied to the coarse-grained allocation decisions made by traffic engineering mechanisms like B4 and SWAN. Exactly where one draws a line between coarse-grain traffic engineering decisions and fine-grain congestion control decisions is not clear, but it's good to keep an open mind about the spectrum of options that are available.

Centralized control has also been used effectively in datacenters, which are an interesting environment for congestion control. First, they have very low RTTs (for traffic between servers in the datacenter, if not for flows heading in or out of the datacenter). Second, in many cases a datacenter can be treated as a greenfield, raising the possibility to try new approaches that don't have to coexist fairly with incumbent algorithms. Fastpass, developed in a collaboration between MIT and Facebook researchers, is a good example of such a centralized approach.

Further Reading:
S. Jain, *et al.* B4: Experience with a Globally-Deployed Software Defined WAN. ACM SIGCOMM, August 2013.

Further Reading:
J. Perry, *et al.* Fastpass: A Centralized "Zero-Queue" Datacenter Network. ACM SIGCOMM, August 2014.

3.1.2 Router-Centric versus Host-Centric

Given a distributed approach to resource allocation, the next question is whether to implement the mechanism inside the network (i.e., at the routers or switches) or at the edges of the network (i.e., in the hosts, perhaps as part of the transport protocol). This is not strictly an either/or situation. Both locations are involved, and the real issue is where the majority of the burden falls. Individual routers always take responsibility for deciding which packets to forward and which packets to drop. However, there is a range of options in how much the router involves the end hosts in specifying how this decision is made, or learning how this decision was made.

At one end of the spectrum, routers can allow hosts to reserve capacity and then ensure each flow's packets are delivered accordingly. They might do this, for example, by implementing a signalling protocol along with Fair Queuing, accepting new flows only when there is sufficient capacity, and policing hosts to make sure their flows stay within their reservations. This would correspond to a reservation-based approach in which the network is able to make QoS guarantees. We consider this out-of-scope for the purpose of this book.

At the other end of the spectrum is a host-centric approach. The router makes no guarantees and offers no explicit feedback about the available capacity (i.e., silently drops packets when its buffers are full) and it is the host's responsibility to observe the network conditions (e.g., how many packets they are successfully getting through the network) and adjust its behavior accordingly.

In the middle, routers can take more proactive action to assist the end hosts in doing their job, but not by reserving buffer space. This involves the router sending *feedback* to the end hosts when its buffers are full. We describe some of these forms of *Active Queue Management (AQM)* in Chapter 6, but the host-centric mechanisms described in the next two chapters assume routers silently tail-drop packets when their buffers are full.

Historically, the host-centric approach has been implemented in the transport layer—usually by TCP, or by some other transport protocol that mimics TCP's algorithm, such as DCCP (datagram congestion control protocol) or QUIC (a relatively recent transport protocol designed for HTTP-based applications). However, it is also possible to implement congestion control in the application itself. *DASH (Dynamic Adaptive Streaming over HTTP)* is an example, although it is best viewed as a combination of congestion control in the transport layer (since it runs over TCP) and the application layer. Based on measured network performance, the server that is streaming video to a client switches among a range of different video encodings, thus changing the rate at which data is sent into the HTTP stream. In effect, TCP tries to find a sustainable bandwidth for the flow, and then the application adapts its sending rate to fully leverage that rate without sending more data than can be sustained under the current network conditions. Primary responsibility for congestion control falls to TCP, but the application aims to keep the pipe full while also maintaining a good user experience.

3.1.3 Window-Based versus Rate-Based

Having settled on a host-centric approach, the next implementation choice is whether the mechanism is *window-based* or *rate-based*. TCP uses a window-based mechanism to implement flow control, so the design decision for TCP congestion control seems obvious. And in fact, the congestion-control mechanisms described in Chapter 4 are centered around an algorithm for computing a *congestion window*, where the sender is throttled by whichever is lesser: the advertised flow-control window or the computed congestion-control window.

But it is also possible to compute the rate at which the network is able to deliver packets, and to pace transmissions accordingly. The observed rate is just the number of bytes delivered over some time period, such as the measured RTT. We point out this duality between rates and windows because a rate-based approach is more appropriate for multimedia applications that generate data at some average rate and which need at least some minimum throughput to be useful. For example, a video codec might generate video at an average rate of 1 Mbps with a peak rate of 2 Mbps.

A rate-based approach is the logical choice in a reservation-based system that supports different QoS levels, but even in a best-effort network like the Internet, it is possible to implement an adaptive rate-based congestion-control mechanism that informs the application when it needs to adjust it transmission rate, for example by adjusting its codec. This is the core idea of TCP-friendly rate control (TFRC), which extends the concepts of TCP congestion avoidance to applications that more naturally send packets at a specific rate (e.g., the bitrate produced by a video codec at a given quality level). TFRC is typically used in conjunction with RTP, a transport protocol designed for real-time applications. We will see examples of such mechanisms in Chapter 7.

Finally, one of the recent advances in TCP congestion control is BBR (Bottleneck Bandwidth and RTT) which uses a combination of window-based and rate-based control, in an effort to limit the build up of queues within the network. We examine this approach in some detail in Chapter 5.

3.1.4 Control-based versus Avoidance-based

The final implementation choice we draw attention to is somewhat subtle. The challenge is for the end-host, based on feedback and observations, to compute how much capacity is available in the network, and adjust its sending rate accordingly. There are two general strategies for doing this: an aggressive approach that purposely sends packets at a rate that causes packet loss and then responds to it, and a conservative approach that tries to detect the onset of queue build-up and slow down before they actually overflow. We refer to the mechanisms of the first type as *control-based*, and we refer to mechanisms of the second type as *avoidance-based*.

This distinction was first called out by Raj Jain and K.K. Ramakrishnan Jain in 1988. It is often overlooked—and the term "congestion control" is used generically to refer to both—but our take is that the distinction represents an important difference, and so we will call it out when appropriate. Admittedly, we will also fall back to the generic use of "congestion control" when the distinction is not critical to the discussion.

Also note that the approaches we call "control-based" and "avoidance-based" are sometimes referred to as *loss-based* and *delay-based*, respectively, according to the criteria each uses as a signal that the congestion window needs to be adjusted. The former adjusts the window when it detects a loss and the latter adjusts the window when it detects a change in the delay gradient. When viewed from this perspective, each of the algorithms introduced over the next four chapters effectively refines the fidelity of these signals in one way or another.

Further Reading:
R. Jain and K. K. Ramakrishnan. Congestion Avoidance in Computer Networks with a Connectionless Network Layer: Concepts, Goals and Methodology.. Computer Networking Symposium, April 1988.

3.2 Evaluation Criteria

Having identified the set of design decisions that go into crafting a congestion-control mechanism, the next question is whether any given solution is good or not. Recall that in Chapter 1 we posed the question of how a network *effectively* and *fairly* allocates its resources. This suggests at least two broad measures by which a resource allocation scheme can be evaluated. We consider each in turn.

3.2.1 Effectiveness

A good starting point for evaluating the effectiveness of a congestion-control mechanism is to consider the two principal metrics of networking: throughput and delay. Clearly, we want as much throughput and as little delay as possible. Unfortunately, these goals can be at odds with each other. One way to increase throughput is to allow as many packets into the network as possible, so as to drive the utilization of all the links up to 100%. We would do this to avoid the possibility of a link becoming idle because an idle link hurts throughput. The problem with this strategy is that increasing the number of packets in the network also increases the length of the queues at each router. Such *persistent queues* mean packets are delayed in the network, or worse, dropped. Having to drop packets in the middle of the network not only impacts delay but also hurts throughput because upstream link bandwidth has been wasted on a packet that was not successfully delivered all the way to the destination.[2]

The ratio of throughput to delay is a general metric for evaluating the effectiveness of a resource allocation scheme. This ratio is sometimes referred to as the *power* of the system:

$$\text{Power} = \text{Throughput}/\text{Delay}$$

Intuitively, the objective is to maximize this ratio, which is a function of how much load you place on the system. The load, in turn, is set by the resource allocation mechanism. Figure 11 gives a representative power curve, where, ideally, the resource allocation mechanism would operate at the peak of this curve. To the left of the peak, the mechanism is being too conservative; that is, it is not allowing enough packets to be sent to keep the links busy. To the right of the peak, so many packets are being allowed into the network that either (a) increases in delay (denominator) due to queuing are starting to dominate any small gains in throughput, or (b) throughput (numerator) actually starts to drop due to packets being dropped.

Moreover, we need to be concerned about what happens even when the system is operating under heavy load—towards the right end of the curve in Figure 11. Ideally, we would like to avoid the situation

[2] We sometimes use the term *goodput* instead of *throughput* to emphasize that we care about data that is successfully delivered through the network to the receiver, as opposed to just transmitted by the sender.

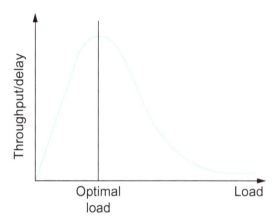

Figure 11: Ratio of throughput to delay as a function of load.

in which the system throughput approaches zero. The goal is for the mechanism to be *stable*—where packets continue to get through the network even when it is operating under heavy load. If a mechanism is not stable under heavy load, the network will suffer from *congestion collapse*.

Note that while both "persistent queues" and "congestion collapse" are to be avoided, there is no precise definition for the threshold at which a network suffers from either. They are both subjective judgments about an algorithm's behavior, where latency and throughput are the two performance indicators that matter.

3.2.2 *Fairness*

The effective utilization of network resources is not the only criterion for judging a resource allocation scheme. We must also consider the issue of fairness. However, we quickly get into murky waters when we try to define what exactly constitutes fair resource allocation. For example, a reservation-based resource allocation scheme provides an explicit way to create controlled unfairness. With such a scheme, we might use reservations to enable a video stream to receive 1 Mbps across some link while a file transfer receives only 10 kbps over the same link.

In the absence of explicit information to the contrary, when several flows share a particular link, we would like for each flow to receive an equal share of the bandwidth. This definition presumes that a *fair* share of bandwidth means an *equal* share of bandwidth. But, even in the absence of reservations, equal shares may not equate to fair shares. Should we also consider the length of the paths being compared? For example, as illustrated in Figure 12, what is fair when one four-hop flow is competing with three one-hop flows?

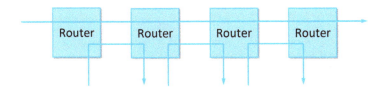

Figure 12: One four-hop flow competing with three one-hop flows.

Assuming that the most fair situation would be one in which all flows receive the same bandwidth, networking researcher Raj Jain proposed a metric that can be used to quantify the fairness of a congestion-control mechanism. Jain's fairness index is defined as follows. Given a set of flow throughputs

$$(x_1, x_2, \ldots, x_n)$$

(measured in consistent units such as bits/second), the following function assigns a fairness index to the flows:

$$f(x_1, x_2, \ldots, x_n) = \frac{\left(\sum_{i=1}^{n} x_i\right)^2}{n \sum_{i=1}^{n} x_i^2}$$

The fairness index always results in a number between 0 and 1, with 1 representing greatest fairness. To understand the intuition behind this metric, consider the case where all n flows receive a throughput of 1 unit of data per second. We can see that the fairness index in this case is

$$\frac{n^2}{n \times n} = 1$$

Now, suppose one flow receives a throughput of $1 + \Delta$. Now the fairness index is

$$\frac{((n-1) + 1 + \Delta)^2}{n(n - 1 + (1 + \Delta)^2)} = \frac{n^2 + 2n\Delta + \Delta^2}{n^2 + 2n\Delta + n\Delta^2}$$

Note that the denominator exceeds the numerator by $(n-1)\Delta^2$. Thus, whether the odd flow out was getting more or less than all the other flows (positive or negative Δ), the fairness index has now dropped below one. Another simple case to consider is where only k of the n flows receive equal throughput, and the remaining n-k users receive zero throughput, in which case the fairness index drops to k/n.

In the next section we revisit the notion of fairness as it applies to the deployment of new congestion control algorithms. As noted above, it is not as clear-cut as it might first appear.

TCP-friendly rate control (TFRC) also uses the notion of fairness. TFRC uses the TCP throughput equation (discussed in Section 1.3) to estimate the share of a congested link's bandwidth that would be obtained by a flow that implemented TCP's congestion control scheme, and sets that as a target rate for an application to send data. The application can then make decisions to help it hit that target rate. For example, a video streaming application might choose among a set of different encoding quality levels to try to maintain an average rate at the "fair" level as determined by TFRC.

Further Reading:
R. Jain, D. Chiu, and W. Hawe. A Quantitative Measure of Fairness and Discrimination for Resource Allocation in Shared Computer Systems. DEC Research Report TR-301, 1984.

3.3 Comparative Analysis

The first step in evaluating any congestion control mechanism is to measure its performance in isolation, including:

- The average throughput (goodput) flows are able to achieve.

- The average end-to-end delay flows experience.

- That the mechanism avoid persistent queues across a range of operating scenarios.

- That the mechanism be stable across a range of operating scenarios.

- The degree to which flows receive a fair share of the available capacity.

The inevitable second step is to compare two or more mechanisms. This is because, given the decentralized nature of the Internet, there is no way to ensure uniform adoption of just one mechanism. Comparing quantitative metrics like throughput is easy. The problem is how to evaluate multiple mechanisms that might coexist, competing with each other for network resources.

The question is not whether a given mechanism treats all of its flows fairly, but whether mechanism A is fair to flows managed by mechanism B. If mechanism A is able to measure improved throughput over B, but it does so by being more aggressive, and hence, stealing bandwidth from B's flows, then A's improvement is not fairly gained and may be discounted. It should be evident that the Internet's highly decentralized approach to congestion control works because a large number of flows respond in a cooperative way to congestion, which opens the door to more aggressive flows improving their performance at the expense of those which implement the accepted, less aggressive algorithms.

Arguments like this have been made many times over the last 30 years, which has raised a high bar to the deployment of new algorithms. Even if global deployment of a new algorithm would be a net positive, incremental deployment (which is the only real option) could negatively impact flows using existing algorithms, leading to a reluctance to deploy new approaches. But such analysis suffers from three problems, as identified by Ranysha Ware and colleagues:

Further Reading:
R. Ware, *et al*. Beyond Jain's Fairness Index: Setting the Bar for the Deployment of Congestion Control Algorithms. ACM SIGCOMM HotNets. November 2019.

- **Ideal-Driven Goalposting:** A fairness-based threshold asserts new mechanism B should equally share the bottleneck link with currently deployed mechanism A. This goal is too idealistic in practice, especially when A is sometimes unfair to its own flows.

- **Throughput-Centricity:** A fairness-based threshold focuses on how new mechanism B impacts a competitor flow using mechanism A by focusing on A's achieved throughput. However, this ignores other important figures of merit for good performance, such as latency, flow completion time, or loss rate.

- **Assumption of Balance:** Inter-mechanism interactions often have some bias, but a fairness metric cannot tell whether the outcome is biased for or against the status quo. It makes a difference in terms of deployability whether a new mechanism B takes a larger share of bandwidth than legacy mechanism A or leaves a larger share for A to consume: the former might elicit complaints from legacy users of A, where the latter would not. Jain's Fairness Index assigns an equivalent score to both scenarios.

Instead of a simple calculation of Jain's fairness index, Ware advocates for a threshold based on *harm*, as measured by a reduction in throughput or an increase in latency or jitter. Intuitively, if the amount of harm caused by flows using a new mechanism B on flows using existing mechanism A is within a bound derived from how much harm A-managed flows cause other A-managed flows, we can consider B deployable alongside A without harm. Ware goes on to propose concrete measures of acceptable harm, which turns out to be more complicated than it might first appear. Even with a single congestion control algorithm, the amount of harm that one flow causes another depends on factors such as its RTT, start time, and duration. Thus measures of harm need to take into account the range of impacts that different flows have on each other under the existing regime and aim to do no worse with a new algorithm.

3.4 Experimental Methodology

Our approach to evaluating congestion-control mechanisms is to measure their performance on real systems, and as we pointed out in Chapter 1, the *de facto* specification of the respective mechanisms is the version implemented in Linux. We now describe one specific way to perform those measurements, illustrating one methodology that is widely practiced today. Our approach uses *Netesto (Network Test Toolkit)*, a collection of software tools available on GitHub. The alternative is simulation-based, with NS-3 being the most popular open source tool.

Note that while the experiments described in this section measure real congestion control algorithms (which, of course, we have not yet described in any detail), the intent is to outline how algorithms are evaluated, and not to actually draw any conclusions about specific mechanisms.

Further Reading:
Netesto.
(https://github.com/facebook/fbkutils)

NS-3 Network Simulator.
(https://www.nsnam.org)

3.4.1 *Experimental Setup*

Our approach uses real TCP senders/receivers running on Linux hosts, with a range of behaviors studied using a combination of kernel packages like netem and tbf qdisc. Performance data is then collected using tcpdump. The network connecting the end-hosts is constructed from a combination of real switches and emulated elements, supporting for example, wide-area delays and low-bandwidth links.

The experiments can be characterized along two orthogonal dimensions. One is the topology of the network. This includes link bandwidths, RTTs, buffer sizes, and so on. The other dimension is the traffic workload we run on the network. This includes the number and duration of flows, as well as the characteristics of each flow (e.g., stream vs. RPC).

With respect to network topology, we evaluate algorithms on three specific configurations:

- LAN with $20\mu s$ RTT and 10-Gbps link bandwidth. This scenario represents servers in the same datacenter rack.

- WAN with 10ms RTT and 10-Gbps link bandwidth, with delay introduced on the receiver by configuring a 20,000 packet send queue. The bottleneck is a real switch with shallow buffers (1-2 MB). This is a good scenario to visualize the algorithm's dynamics when looking at two to three flows.

- WAN with 40ms RTT and 10/100-Mbps bottleneck bandwidth, with an intermediate router introduced to reduce the link bandwidth to 10 or 100 Mbps. This scenario reflects a connection an end-user might experience on a modern network.

Figure 13 shows the topology for the first two scenarios, where the senders and receivers are connected through a single switch. Delay is achieved for the second scenario using netem in the Receiver, which affects only the ACKs being sent back.

Figure 14 shows the topology for the third scenario, where the router is implemented by a server-based forwarder that throttles outgoing link bandwidth using tbf qdisc.

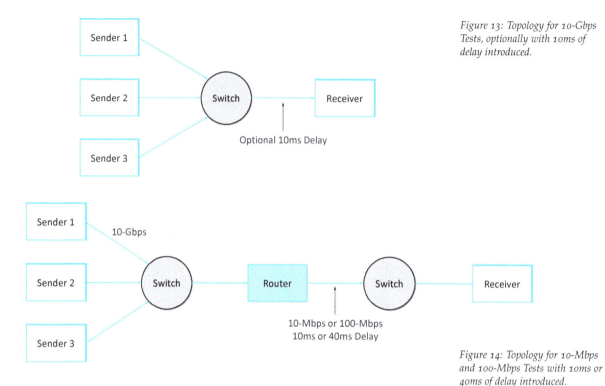

Figure 13: Topology for 10-Gbps Tests, optionally with 10ms of delay introduced.

Figure 14: Topology for 10-Mbps and 100-Mbps Tests with 10ms or 40ms of delay introduced.

With respect to traffic workload, we evaluate the dynamics and fairness of algorithms with the following tests:

- 2-flow Test: The first flow lasts 60 seconds, and the second flow lasts 20 seconds and starts 22 seconds after the first one.

- 3-flow Test: The first flow lasts 60 seconds, the second flow lasts 40 seconds and starts 12 seconds after the first one, the third flow lasts 20 seconds and starts 26 seconds after the first one.

These tests make it possible to:

- Examine how quickly existing flows adapt to new flows.

- Examine how quickly flows adapt to released bandwidth from terminating flows.

- Measure fairness between flows with the same (or different) congestion algorithm(s).

- Measure levels of congestion.

- Identify conditions under which performance changes abruptly, signalling a possible instability.

Additional tests include a combination of streaming, plus 10-KB and 1-MB RPCs. These tests allow us to see if the smaller RPC flows are penalized, and if so, by how much. These tests make it possible to:

- Study behavior under increasing loads.

- Measure the performance (throughput and latency) of 1-MB and 10-KB flows, as well as how fairly is the available bandwidth divided between them.

- Identify conditions when the retransmissions or latency change abruptly, signalling an instability.

3.4.2 Example Results

The following shows some example results, selected to illustrate the evaluation process. We start with a simple 2-flow experiment, where both flows are managed by the same congestion-control algorithm. Figure 15 shows the resulting goodput graph. As one would hope, once the second flow (in red) starts just after 20 seconds, the goodput of both flows converge towards a nearly equal sharing of the available bandwidth. This convergence is not immediate (the two plots cross over roughly ten seconds after the second flow begins), a behavior other algorithms try to correct (e.g., by using explicit feedback from routers). On the plus side, the first flow does quickly adapt to the released bandwidth once the second flow terminates.

It is also possible to look more closely at these two flows, for example, by tracking the congestion window for each. The corresponding plot is shown in Figure 16. Not surprisingly, different algorithms would have different "patterns" to congestion windows over time, as we will see in the next chapter.

We could repeat these experiments but vary the algorithm used by one of the flows. This would allow us to visualize how the two algorithms interact. If they are both fair, you would expect to see

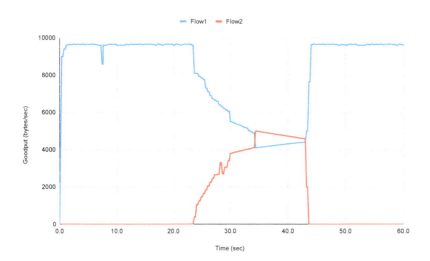

Figure 15: Goodput (bytes per second delivered end-to-end) realized by two flows running under the same congestion-control algorithm.

results similar to Figure 15. If not, you might see a graph similar to Figure 17, in which the second flow (Algorithm B) aggressively takes bandwidth away from the first flow (Algorithm A).

These experiments can be repeated with three concurrent flows, but we turn next to evaluating how various algorithms treat different workloads. In particular, we are interested in the question of *size fairness*, that is, how a given algorithm treats back-to-back 10-KB or 1-MB RPC calls when they have to compete with ongoing stream-based flows. Some example results are shown in Figure 18 (1-MB RPCs) and Figure 19 (10-KB RPCs). The figures show the performance of five different algorithms (represented by different colors), across test runs with 1, 2, 4, 8, and 16 concurrent streaming flows.

The 1-MB results are unsurprising, with no significant outliers across the five algorithms, and the average goodput decreasing as the RPCs compete with more and more streams. Although not shown in Figure 18, the fourth algorithm (green), which performs best when all flows are stream-based, suffers a significant number of retransmissions when sharing the available bandwidth among RPC calls.

The 10-KB results do have a significant outlier, with the third algorithm (yellow) performing significantly better; by a factor of 4x. If

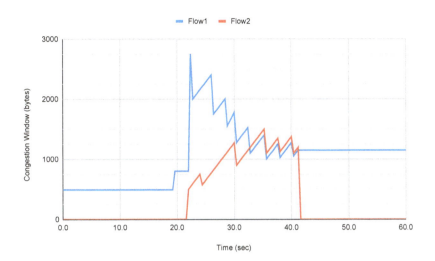

Figure 16: Congestion window (measured in bytes) for two flows competing for bandwidth under the same congestion-control algorithm.

you plot latency rather than bandwidth—the more relevant metric for small-message RPC calls—it turns out the third algorithm both achieves the lowest latencies and does so consistently, with the 99th and 99.9-th percentiles being the same.

Finally, all of the preceding experiments can be repeated on a network topology that includes wide-area RTTs. Certainly inter-flow fairness and size fairness continue to be concerns, but there is also an increased likelihood that queuing delays become an issue. For example, Figure 20 shows the 99% latencies for four different algorithms when the network topology includes a 10-Mbps bottleneck link and a 40ms RTT. One important observation about this result is that the second algorithm (red) performs poorly when there is less than one bandwidth-delay product of buffering available at the bottleneck router, calling attention to another variable that can influence your results.

We conclude this discussion of experimental methodology by permitting ourselves one summary evaluation statement. When looking across a set of algorithms and a range of topology/traffic scenarios, we conclude that: *No single algorithm is better than all other algorithms under all conditions.* One explanation, as these examples demonstrate,

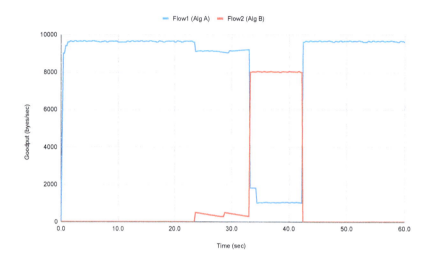

Figure 17: Goodput (bytes per second delivered end-to-end) realized by two flows running under different congestion-control algorithms, with one flow receiving significantly less bandwidth than the other.

is how many factors there are to take into consideration. This also explains why congestion control continues to be a topic of interest for both network researchers and network practitioners.

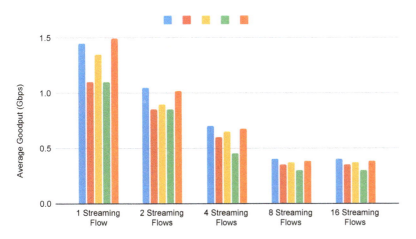

Figure 18: Average goodput (measured in Gbps) realized by a sequence of 1-MB RPC calls for five different algorithms, when competing with a varied number of TCP streams.

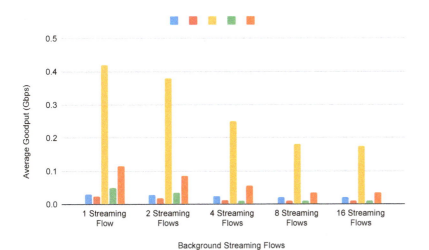

Figure 19: Average goodput (measured in Gbps) realized by a sequence of 10-KB RPC calls for five different algorithms, when competing with a varied number of TCP streams.

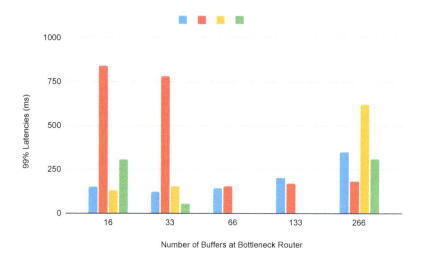

Figure 20: 99th percentile latencies for 10-KB RPC calls when competing with a single streaming flow on a 40ms WAN, measured for a different number of buffers at the bottleneck router.

Chapter 4: Control-Based Algorithms

This chapter describes the dominant congestion-control algorithm in use today on the Internet. The approach was introduced in 1988 by Van Jacobson and Mike Karels, and refined multiple times over the years. The variant in widespread use today is called CUBIC, for reasons that will become clear at the end of the chapter.

The general idea is straightforward. Having transmitted a set of packets according to its current estimate of the available bandwidth, a TCP sender reacts to two signals from the network. On the one hand, the arrival of an ACK signals that one of its packets has left the network and that it is therefore safe to transmit a new packet without adding to the level of congestion. By using ACKs to pace the transmission of packets, TCP is said to be *self-clocking*. On the other hand, a timeout signals that a packet was lost, implying that the network is congested, and thus TCP needs to reduce its sending rate. Because using packet loss as a signal means congestion has already occurred and we are reacting after the fact, we refer to this approach as *control-based*.

There are many subtle issues that must be addressed to make this a practical approach to congestion control. This chapter describes the collection of techniques that address these issues, and as such, can be read as a case study of the experience of identifying and solving a sequence of problems. We will trace the historical context as we visit each of the techniques in the sections that follow.

4.1 Timeout Calculation

Timeouts and retransmissions are a central part TCP's approach to implementing a reliable byte-stream, but timeouts also play a key role in congestion control because they signal packet loss, which in turn indicates the likelihood of congestion. In other words, TCP's timeout mechanism is a building block for its overall approach to congestion control.

Note that a timeout can happen because a packet was lost, or because the corresponding acknowledgment was lost, or because nothing was lost but the ACK took longer to arrive than we were expecting. Hence it is important to know how long it might take an ACK to arrive, because otherwise we risk responding as if there was congestion when there was not.

TCP has an adaptive approach to setting a timeout, computed as a function of the measured RTT. As simple as this sounds, the full implementation is more involved than you might expect, and has been through multiple refinements over the years. This section revisits that experience.

4.1.1 Original Algorithm

We begin with the simple algorithm that was originally described in the TCP specification. The idea is to keep a running average of the RTT and then to compute the timeout as a function of this RTT. Specifically, every time TCP sends a data segment, it records the time. When an ACK for that segment arrives, TCP reads the time again, and then takes the difference between these two times as a SampleRTT. TCP then computes an EstimatedRTT as a weighted average between the previous estimate and this new sample. That is,

$$\text{EstimatedRTT} = \alpha \times \text{EstimatedRTT} + (1 - \alpha) \times \text{SampleRTT}$$

The parameter α is selected to *smooth* the EstimatedRTT. A small α tracks changes in the RTT but is perhaps too heavily influenced by temporary fluctuations. On the other hand, a large α is more stable but perhaps not quick enough to adapt to real changes. The original TCP specification recommended a setting of α between 0.8 and 0.9. TCP then uses EstimatedRTT to compute the timeout in a rather conservative way:

$$\text{TimeOut} = 2 \times \text{EstimatedRTT}$$

4.1.2 Karn/Partridge Algorithm

After several years, a rather obvious flaw was discovered in this simple approach: An ACK does not really acknowledge a transmission, but rather, it acknowledges the receipt of data. In other words, whenever a segment is retransmitted and then an ACK arrives at the sender, it is impossible to determine if this ACK should be associated with the first or the second transmission of the segment for the purpose of measuring the sample RTT.

It is necessary to know which transmission to associate it with so as to compute an accurate SampleRTT. As illustrated in Figure 21, if you assume that the ACK is for the original transmission but it was really for the second, then the SampleRTT is too large (a); if you assume that the ACK is for the second transmission but it was actually for the first, then the SampleRTT is too small (b).

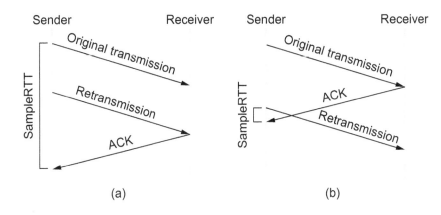

Figure 21: Associating the ACK with (a) original transmission versus (b) retransmission.

The solution at first looks surprisingly simple. It is known as the Karn/Partridge algorithm, after its inventors. With this algorithm, whenever TCP retransmits a segment, it stops taking samples of the

RTT; it only measures SampleRTT for segments that have been sent only once. But the algorithm also includes a second change to TCP's timeout mechanism. Each time TCP retransmits, it sets the next timeout to be twice the last timeout, rather than basing it on the last EstimatedRTT. That is, Karn and Partridge proposed that RTT estimation uses exponential backoff. The motivation for using exponential backoff is that timeouts cause retransmission, and retransmitted segments are no longer contributing to an update in the RTT estimate. So the idea is to be more cautious in declaring that a packet has been lost, rather than getting into a possible cycle of aggressively timing out and then retransmitting. We will see this idea of exponential backoff again, embodied in a much more sophisticated mechanism, in a later section.

4.1.3 Jacobson/Karels Algorithm

The Karn/Partridge algorithm was an improvement to RTT estimation, but it did not eliminate congestion. The 1988 congestion-control mechanism proposed by Jacobson and Karels includes (along with several other components) a new way to decide when to time out and retransmit a segment.

The main problem with the original computation is that it does not take the variance of the sample RTTs into account. Intuitively, if the variation among samples is small, then the EstimatedRTT can be better trusted and there is no reason for multiplying this estimate by 2 to compute the timeout. On the other hand, a large variance in the samples suggests that the timeout value should not be too tightly coupled to the EstimatedRTT.

In the new approach, the sender measures a new SampleRTT as before. It then folds this new sample into the timeout calculation as follows:

$$\text{Difference} = \text{SampleRTT} - \text{EstimatedRTT}$$

$$\text{EstimatedRTT} = \text{EstimatedRTT} + (\delta \times \text{Difference})$$

$$\text{Deviation} = \text{Deviation} + \delta(|\text{Difference}| - \text{Deviation})$$

where δ is between 0 and 1. That is, we calculate both the mean RTT and the variation in that mean. TCP then computes the timeout value as a function of both EstimatedRTT and Deviation as follows:

$$\text{TimeOut} = \mu \times \text{EstimatedRTT} + \phi \times \text{Deviation}$$

where based on experience, μ is typically set to 1 and ϕ is set to 4. Thus, when the variance is small, TimeOut is close to EstimatedRTT; a large variance causes the Deviation term to dominate the calculation.

4.1.4 Implementation

There are two items of note regarding the implementation of timeouts in TCP. The first is that it is possible to implement the calculation for EstimatedRTT and Deviation without using floating-point arithmetic. Instead, the whole calculation is scaled by 2^n, with δ selected to be $1/2^n$. This allows us to do integer arithmetic, implementing multiplication and division using shifts, thereby achieving higher performance. The resulting calculation is given by the following code fragment, where n=3 (i.e., $\delta = 1/8$). Note that EstimatedRTT and Deviation are stored in their scaled-up forms, while the value of SampleRTT at the start of the code and of TimeOut at the end are real, unscaled values. If you find the code hard to follow, you might want to try plugging some real numbers into it and verifying that it gives the same results as the equations above.

```
{
    SampleRTT -= (EstimatedRTT >> 3);
    EstimatedRTT += SampleRTT;
    if (SampleRTT < 0)
        SampleRTT = -SampleRTT;
    SampleRTT -= (Deviation >> 3);
    Deviation += SampleRTT;
    TimeOut = (EstimatedRTT >> 3) + (Deviation >> 1);
}
```

The second is that the algorithm is only as good as the clock used to read the current time. On typical Unix implementations at the time, the clock granularity was as large as 500 ms, which is significantly larger than the average cross-country RTT of somewhere between 100 and 200 ms. To make matters worse, the Unix implementation of TCP only checked to see if a timeout should happen every time this 500-ms clock ticked and would only take a sample of the round-trip time once per RTT. The combination of these two factors could mean that a timeout would happen 1 second after the segment was transmitted. An extension to TCP, described in the next section, makes this RTT calculation a bit more precise. For additional details about the implementation of timeouts in TCP, we refer the reader to the authoritative RFC.

Further Reading:
RFC 6298: Computing TCP's Retransmission Timer. June 2011.

4.1.5 TCP Timestamp Extension

The changes to TCP described up to this point have been adjustments to how the sender computes timeouts, with no changes to the over-the-wire protocol. But there are also extensions to the TCP header that help improve its ability to manage timeouts and retransmissions. We discuss one that relates to RTT estimation here. Another extension, establishing a scaling factor for AdvertisedWindow, was described in Section 2.3., and a third, selective acknowledgment or SACK is discussed below.

The TCP timestamp extension helps to improve TCP's timeout mechanism. Instead of measuring the RTT using a coarse-grained event, TCP can read the actual system clock when it is about to send a segment, and put this time—think of it as a 32-bit *timestamp*—in the segment's header. The receiver then echoes this timestamp back to the sender in its acknowledgment, and the sender subtracts this timestamp from the current time to measure the RTT. In essence, the timestamp option provides a convenient place for TCP to store the record of when a segment was transmitted; it stores the time in the segment itself. Note that the endpoints in the connection do not need synchronized clocks, since the timestamp is written and read at the same end of the connection. This improves the measurement of RTT and hence reduces the risk of incorrect timeouts due to poor RTT estimates.

This timestamp extension serves a second purpose, in that it also provides a way to create a 64-bit sequence number field, addressing the shortcomings of TCP's 32-bit sequence number outlined in Section 2.3. Specifically, TCP decides whether to accept or reject a segment based on a logical 64-bit identifier that has the SequenceNum field in the low-order 32 bits and the timestamp in the high-order 32 bits. Since the timestamp is always increasing, it serves to distinguish between two different incarnations of the same sequence number. Note that the timestamp is being used in this setting only to protect against wraparound; it is not treated as part of the sequence number for the purpose of ordering or acknowledging data.

4.2 Additive Increase/Multiplicative Decrease

A better way to compute timeouts is a necessary building block, but it does not get at the heart of controlling congestion. The central challenge is computing an estimate of how much traffic the network this sender can safely transmit. To this end, TCP maintains a new state variable for each connection, which we refer to as CongestionWindow (but you will often see it called cwnd in the literature, based on the variable name used in the code). It is used by the source to limit how much data it is allowed to have in transit at a given time.

The congestion window is congestion control's counterpart to flow control's advertised window. The TCP sender is modified such that the maximum number of bytes of unacknowledged data allowed is now the minimum of the congestion window and the advertised window. Thus, using the variables defined in Chapter 2, TCP's effective window is revised as follows:

$$MaxWindow = MIN(CongestionWindow, AdvertisedWindow)$$

$$EffectiveWindow = MaxWindow - (LastByteSent - LastByteAcked)$$

That is, MaxWindow replaces AdvertisedWindow in the calculation of EffectiveWindow. Thus, a TCP source is allowed to send no faster than the slowest component—the network or the destination host—can accommodate.

The problem, of course, is how TCP comes to learn an appropriate value for CongestionWindow. Unlike the AdvertisedWindow, which is sent by the receiving side of the connection, there is no one to send a suitable CongestionWindow to the sending side of TCP. The answer is that the TCP source sets the CongestionWindow based on the level of congestion it perceives to exist in the network. This involves decreasing the congestion window when the level of congestion goes up and increasing the congestion window when the level of congestion goes down. Taken together, the mechanism is commonly called *additive increase/multiplicative decrease (AIMD)* due to the approach it adopts.

The key question then becomes: how does the source determine that the network is congested and that it should decrease the congestion window? The answer is based on the observation that the main reason packets are not delivered, and a timeout results, is that a packet was dropped due to congestion. It is rare that a packet is dropped because of an error during transmission. Therefore, TCP interprets timeouts as a sign of congestion and reduces the rate at which it is transmitting. Specifically, each time a timeout occurs, the source sets CongestionWindow to half of its previous value. This halving of the CongestionWindow for each timeout corresponds to the "multiplicative decrease" part of AIMD.

Although CongestionWindow is defined in terms of bytes, it is easiest to understand multiplicative decrease if we think in terms of whole packets. For example, suppose the CongestionWindow is currently set to 16 packets. If a loss is detected, CongestionWindow is set to 8. (Normally, a loss is detected when a timeout occurs, but as we see below, TCP has another mechanism to detect dropped packets.) Additional losses cause CongestionWindow to be reduced to 4, then 2, and finally to 1 packet. CongestionWindow is not allowed to fall below the size of a single packet, which we know from Chapter 2 to be the MSS.

A congestion-control strategy that only decreases the window size is obviously too conservative. We also need to be able to increase the congestion window to take advantage of newly available capacity in the network. This is the "additive increase" part of AIMD, and it works as follows. Every time the source successfully sends a CongestionWindow's worth of packets—that is, each packet sent out during the

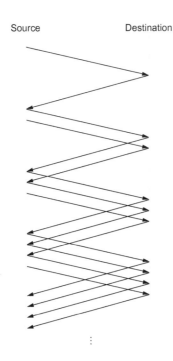

Source   Destination

Figure 22: Packets in transit during additive increase, with one packet being added each RTT.

last round-trip time (RTT) has been ACKed—it adds the equivalent of 1 packet to CongestionWindow. This linear increase is illustrated in Figure 22.

In practice, TCP does not wait for an entire window's worth of ACKs to add 1 packet's worth to the congestion window, but instead increments CongestionWindow by a little for each ACK that arrives. Specifically, the congestion window is incremented as follows each time an ACK arrives:

$$\text{Increment} = \text{MSS} \times (\text{MSS} / \text{CongestionWindow})$$

$$\text{CongestionWindow} = \text{CongestionWindow} + \text{Increment}$$

That is, rather than incrementing CongestionWindow by an entire MSS bytes each RTT, we increment it by a fraction of MSS every time an ACK is received. Assuming that each ACK acknowledges the receipt of MSS bytes, then that fraction is MSS/CongestionWindow.

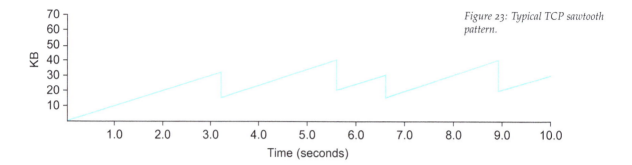

Figure 23: Typical TCP sawtooth pattern.

This pattern of continually increasing and decreasing the congestion window continues throughout the lifetime of the connection. In fact, if you plot the current value of CongestionWindow as a function of time, you get a sawtooth pattern, as illustrated in Figure 23. The important concept to understand about AIMD is that the source is willing to reduce its congestion window at a much faster rate than it is willing to increase its congestion window. One could imagine an additive increase/additive decrease strategy in which the window would be increased by 1 packet when an ACK arrives and decreased by 1 when a timeout occurs, but this turns out to be too aggressive. Responding quickly to congestion is important to stability.

An intuitive explanation for why TCP decreases the window aggressively and increases it conservatively is that the consequences of having too large a window are compounding. This is because when the window is too large, packets that are dropped will be retransmitted, making congestion even worse. It is important to get out of this state quickly. You can think of AIMD as gently increasing the data in flight to probe for the level at which congestion begins, then aggressively stepping back from the brink of congestion collapse when that level is detected by a timeout.

Finally, since a timeout is an indication of congestion that triggers multiplicative decrease, TCP needs the most accurate timeout mechanism it can afford. We already covered TCP's timeout mechanism in Section 4.1, but two main things to remember about that mechanism are that (1) timeouts are set as a function of both the average RTT and the standard deviation in that average, and (2) due to the cost of measuring each transmission with an accurate clock, TCP only samples the round-trip time once per RTT (rather than once per packet) using a coarse-grained (500-ms) clock.

4.3 Slow Start

The additive increase mechanism just described is a reasonable approach to use when the source is operating close to the available capacity of the network, but it takes too long to ramp up a connection when it is starting from scratch. TCP therefore provides a second mechanism, counter-intuitively called *slow start*, which is used to increase the congestion window rapidly from a cold start. Slow start effectively increases the congestion window exponentially, rather than linearly.

Specifically, the source starts out by setting CongestionWindow to one packet. When the ACK for this packet arrives, TCP adds 1 to CongestionWindow and then sends two packets. Upon receiving the corresponding two ACKs, TCP increments CongestionWindow by 2—one for each ACK—and next sends four packets. The end result is that TCP effectively doubles the number of packets it has in transit every RTT. Figure 24 shows the growth in the number of packets in transit during slow start. Compare this to the linear growth of additive increase illustrated in Figure 22.

Why any exponential mechanism would be called "slow" is puzzling at first, but it makes sense in its historical context. We need to compare slow start not against the linear mechanism of the previous section, but against the original behavior of TCP. Consider what happens when a connection is established and the source first starts to send packets—that is, when it currently has no packets in transit. If the source sends as many packets as the advertised window allows—which is exactly what TCP did before slow start was developed—then even if there is a fairly large amount of bandwidth available in the network, the routers may not be able to consume this burst of packets. It all depends on how much buffer space is available at the routers. Slow start was therefore designed to space packets out so that this burst does not occur. In other words, even though its exponential

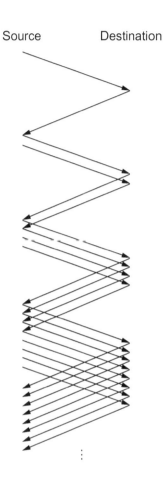

Source   Destination

Figure 24: Packets in transit during slow start.

growth is faster than linear growth, slow start is much "slower" than sending an entire advertised window's worth of data all at once.

There are actually two different situations in which slow start runs. The first is at the very beginning of a connection, at which time the source has no idea how many packets it is going to be able to have in transit at a given time. (Keep in mind that today TCP runs over everything from 1-Mbps links to 40-Gbps links, so there is no way for the source to know the network's capacity.) In this situation, slow start continues to double CongestionWindow each RTT until there is a loss, at which time a timeout causes multiplicative decrease to divide CongestionWindow by 2.

The second situation in which slow start is used is a bit more subtle; it occurs when the connection goes dead while waiting for a timeout to occur. Recall how TCP's sliding window algorithm works—when a packet is lost, the source eventually reaches a point where it has sent as much data as the advertised window allows, and so it blocks while waiting for an ACK that will not arrive. Eventually, a timeout happens, but by this time there are no packets in transit, meaning that the source will receive no ACKs to "clock" the transmission of new packets. The source will instead receive a single cumulative ACK that reopens the entire advertised window, but, as explained above, the source then uses slow start to restart the flow of data rather than dumping a whole window's worth of data on the network all at once.

Although the source is using slow start again, it now knows more information than it did at the beginning of a connection. Specifically, the source has a current (and useful) value of CongestionWindow; this is the value of CongestionWindow that existed prior to the last packet loss, divided by 2 as a result of the loss. We can think of this as the *target* congestion window. Slow start is used to rapidly increase the sending rate up to this value, and then additive increase is used beyond this point. Notice that we have a small bookkeeping problem to take care of, in that we want to remember the target congestion window resulting from multiplicative decrease as well as the *actual* congestion window being used by slow start. To address this problem, TCP introduces a temporary variable to store the target window, typically called CongestionThreshold, that is set equal to the CongestionWindow value that results from multiplicative decrease. The variable CongestionWindow is then reset to one packet, and it is incremented by one packet for every ACK that is received until it reaches CongestionThreshold, at which point it is incremented by one packet per RTT.

In other words, TCP increases the congestion window as defined by the following code fragment where state represents the state of a particular TCP connection and defines an upper bound on how large the congestion window is allowed to grow.

```
{
    u_int    cw = state->CongestionWindow;
    u_int    incr = state->maxseg;

    if (cw > state->CongestionThreshold)
        incr = incr * incr / cw;
    state->CongestionWindow = MIN(cw + incr, TCP_MAXWIN);
}
```

Figure 25 traces how TCP's CongestionWindow increases and decreases over time and serves to illustrate the interplay of slow start and additive increase/multiplicative decrease. This trace was taken from an actual TCP connection and shows the current value of CongestionWindow—the colored line—over time.

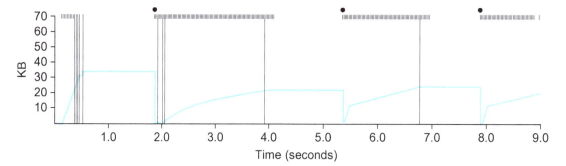

There are several things to notice about this trace. The first is the rapid increase in the congestion window at the beginning of the connection. This corresponds to the initial slow start phase. The slow start phase continues until several packets are lost at about 0.4 seconds into the connection, at which time CongestionWindow flattens out at about 34 KB. (Why so many packets are lost during slow start is discussed below.) The reason why the congestion window flattens is that there are no ACKs arriving, due to the fact that several packets were lost. In fact, no new packets are sent during this time, as denoted by the lack of hash marks at the top of the graph. A timeout eventually happens at approximately 2 seconds, at which time the congestion window is divided by 2 (i.e., cut from approximately 34 KB to around 17 KB) and

Figure 25: Behavior of TCP congestion control. Colored line = value of CongestionWindow over time; solid bullets at top of graph = timeouts; hash marks at top of graph = time when each packet is transmitted; vertical bars = time when a packet that is eventually retransmitted was first transmitted.

CongestionThreshold is set to this value. Slow start then causes CongestionWindow to be reset to one packet and to start ramping up from there.

There is not enough detail in the trace to see exactly what happens when a couple of packets are lost just after 2 seconds, so we jump ahead to the linear increase in the congestion window that occurs between 2 and 4 seconds. This corresponds to additive increase. At about 4 seconds, CongestionWindow flattens out, again due to a lost packet. Now, at about 5.5 seconds:

1. A timeout happens, causing the congestion window to be divided by 2, dropping it from approximately 22 KB to 11 KB, and CongestionThreshold is set to this amount.

2. CongestionWindow is reset to one packet, as the sender enters slow start.

3. Slow start causes CongestionWindow to grow exponentially until it reaches CongestionThreshold.

4. CongestionWindow then grows linearly.

The same pattern is repeated at around 8 seconds when another timeout occurs.

We now return to the question of why so many packets are lost during the initial slow start period. At this point, TCP is attempting to learn how much bandwidth is available on the network. This is a difficult task. If the source is not aggressive at this stage—for example, if it only increases the congestion window linearly—then it takes a long time for it to discover how much bandwidth is available. This can have a dramatic impact on the throughput achieved for this connection. On the other hand, if the source is aggressive at this stage, as TCP is during exponential growth, then the source runs the risk of having half a window's worth of packets dropped by the network.

To see what can happen during exponential growth, consider the situation in which the source was just able to successfully send 16 packets through the network, causing it to double its congestion window to 32. Suppose, however, that the network happens to have just enough capacity to support 16 packets from this source. The likely result is that 16 of the 32 packets sent under the new congestion window will be dropped by the network; actually, this is the worst-case outcome, since some of the packets will be buffered in some router. This problem will become increasingly severe as the bandwidth-delay product of networks increases. For example, a bandwidth-delay product of 1.8 MB means that each connection has the potential to lose up to 1.8 MB of data at the beginning of each connection. Of course, this assumes that both the source and the destination implement the "big windows" extension.

Alternatives to slow start, whereby the source tries to estimate the available bandwidth by more sophisticated means, have also been explored. One example is called *quick-start*. The basic idea is that a TCP sender can ask for an initial sending rate greater than slow start would allow by putting a requested rate in its SYN packet as an IP option. Routers along the path can examine the option, evaluate the current level of congestion on the outgoing link for this flow, and decide if that rate is acceptable, if a lower rate would be acceptable, or if standard slow start should be used. By the time the SYN reaches the receiver, it will contain either a rate that was acceptable to all routers on the path or an indication that one or more routers on the path could not support the quick-start request. In the former case, the TCP sender uses that rate to begin transmission; in the latter case, it falls back to standard slow start. If TCP is allowed to start off sending at a higher rate, a session could more quickly reach the point of filling the pipe, rather than taking many round-trip times to do so.

Clearly one of the challenges to this sort of enhancement to TCP is that it requires substantially more cooperation from the routers than standard TCP does. If a single router in the path does not support quick-start, then the system reverts to standard slow start. Thus, it could be a long time before these types of enhancements could make it into the Internet; for now, they are more likely to be used in controlled network environments (e.g., research networks).

4.4 Fast Retransmit and Fast Recovery

The mechanisms described so far were part of the original proposal to add congestion control to TCP, and they have collectively become known as *TCP Tahoe* because they were included in the *Tahoe* release of 4.3 BSD Unix in 1988. Once widely deployed, experience revealed some problems in Tahoe that were subsequently addressed by *TCP Reno* (part of the 4.3BSD-Reno release) in early 1990. This section describes that experience and Reno's approach to addressing it.

In short, the coarse-grained implementation of TCP timeouts led to long periods of time during which the connection went dead while waiting for a timer to expire. A heuristic, called *fast retransmit*, sometimes triggers the retransmission of a dropped packet sooner than the regular timeout mechanism. The fast retransmit mechanism does not replace regular timeouts; it just adds another way of detecting lost packets that can be more timely.

The idea is that every time a data packet arrives at the receiving side, the receiver responds with an acknowledgment, even if this sequence number has already been acknowledged. Thus, when a packet arrives out of order—when TCP cannot yet acknowledge the data the packet contains because earlier data has not yet arrived—TCP resends the same acknowledgment it sent the last time.

This second transmission of the same acknowledgment is called a *duplicate ACK*. When the sending side sees a duplicate ACK, it knows that the other side must have received a packet out of order, which suggests that an earlier packet might have been lost. Since it is also possible that the earlier packet has only been delayed rather than lost, the sender waits until it sees some number of duplicate ACKs (in practice, three) and then retransmits the missing packet. The built-in assumption here, which is well tested in practice, is that out-of-order packets are less common by far than lost packets.

Figure 26 illustrates how duplicate ACKs lead to a fast retransmit. In this example, the destination receives packets 1 and 2, but packet 3 is lost in the network. Thus, the destination will send a duplicate ACK for packet 2 when packet 4 arrives, again when packet 5 arrives, and so on. (To simplify this example, we think in terms of packets

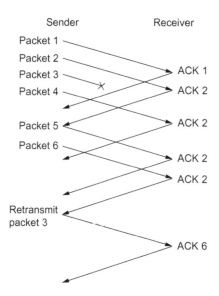

Figure 26: Fast retransmit based on duplicate ACKs.

1, 2, 3, and so on, rather than worrying about the sequence numbers for each byte.) When the sender sees the third duplicate ACK for packet 2—the one sent because the receiver had gotten packet 6—it retransmits packet 3. Note that when the retransmitted copy of packet 3 arrives at the destination, the receiver then sends a cumulative ACK for everything up to and including packet 6 back to the source.

Figure 27 illustrates the behavior of a version of TCP with the fast retransmit mechanism. It is interesting to compare this trace with that given in Figure 25, where fast retransmit was not implemented—the long periods during which the congestion window stays flat and no packets are sent have been eliminated. In general, this technique is able to eliminate about half of the coarse-grained timeouts on a typical TCP connection, resulting in roughly a 20% improvement in the throughput over what could otherwise have been achieved. Notice, however, that the fast retransmit strategy does not eliminate all coarse-grained timeouts. This is because for a small window size there will not be enough packets in transit to cause enough duplicate ACKs to be delivered. Given enough lost packets—for example, as happens during the initial slow start phase—the sliding window algorithm eventually blocks the sender until a timeout occurs. In practice, TCP's fast retransmit mechanism can detect up to three dropped packets per window.

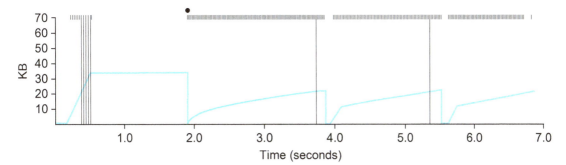

Figure 27: Trace of TCP with fast retransmit. Colored line = CongestionWindow; solid bullet = timeout; hash marks = time when each packet is transmitted; vertical bars = time when a packet that was eventually retransmitted was first transmitted.

There is one further improvement we can make. When the fast retransmit mechanism signals congestion, rather than drop the congestion window all the way back to one packet and run slow start, it is possible to use the ACKs that are still in the pipe to clock the sending of packets. This mechanism is called *fast recovery*, and it effectively removes the slow start phase that happens between when fast retransmit detects a lost packet and additive increase begins. For example, fast recovery avoids the slow start period between 3.8 and 4 seconds in Figure 27 and instead simply cuts the congestion window in half (from 22 KB to 11 KB) and resumes additive increase. This means slow start is used only at the beginning of a connection and whenever a coarse-grained timeout occurs. At all other times, the congestion window follows a pure additive increase/multiplicative decrease pattern.

4.5 Incremental Enhancements

If a study of TCP congestion control teaches us one thing, it's how complex the problem is, and how many details you have to get right. This happens only through a sequence of incremental improvements that are the result of experience. The following gives two additional examples of that lesson.

4.5.1 TCP SACK

The original TCP specification uses cumulative acknowledgments, meaning that the receiver acknowledges the last packet it received prior to any lost packets. You can think of the receiver having a collection of received packets where any lost packets are represented by holes in the received byte stream. With the original specification, it's only possible to tell the sender where the first hole starts, even if several packets have been lost. Intuitively, this lack of detail could limit the sender's ability to respond effectively to packet loss. The approach taken to address this is called *selective acknowledgments* or *SACK*. SACK is another optional extension to TCP that was first proposed soon after the early work of Jacobson and Karels but took some years to gain acceptance, as it was hard to prove that it would be beneficial.

Without SACK, there are only two reasonable strategies for a sender to adopt when segments are received out-of-order. The pessimistic strategy responds to a duplicate ACK or a timeout by retransmitting not just the segment that was clearly lost (the first packet missing at the receiver), but any segments transmitted subsequently. In effect, the pessimistic strategy assumes the worst: that all those segments were lost. The disadvantage of the pessimistic strategy is that it may unnecessarily retransmit segments that were successfully received the first time. The other strategy is to respond to a loss signal (timeout or duplicate ACK) by retransmitting only the segment that triggered that signal. This optimistic approach assumes the rosiest scenario: that only the one segment has been lost. The disadvantage of the optimistic strategy is that it is very slow to recover when a series of consecutive segments has been lost, as might happen when there is congestion. It is slow because each segment's loss is not discovered until the sender receives an ACK for its retransmission of the previous segment. This means it consumes one RTT per segment until it has retransmitted all the segments in the lost series. With the SACK option, a better strategy is available to the sender: retransmit just the segments that fill the gaps between the segments that have been selectively acknowledged.

SACK is first negotiated at the start of a connection by the sender telling the receiver that it can handle the SACK option. When the SACK option is used, the receiver continues to acknowledge segments normally—the meaning of the Acknowledge field does not change—but it also extends the header with additional acknowledgments for any blocks received out-of-order. This allows the sender to identify the holes that exist at the receiver, and retransmit just the segments that are missing instead of all the segments that follow a dropped segment.

SACK was shown to improve the performance of TCP Reno particularly in the case where multiple packets were dropped in a single RTT, as would be expected (since cumulative ACK and SACK are the same thing when only one packet is dropped). This scenario became more likely over time as bandwidth-delay products increased, leaving more packets in the pipe for a given RTT. Hence SACK, which became a proposed IETF standard in 1996, was a timely addition to TCP.

4.5.2 NewReno

Starting with some research by Janey Hoe at MIT in the mid-1990s, the enhancement known as *NewReno* incrementally improves the performance of TCP by making more intelligent decisions about which packets to retransmit under certain packet loss conditions.

The key insight behind NewReno is that even without SACK, duplicate ACKs can convey information to the sender about how many packets have been dropped and which ones they were, so that the sender can make more intelligent choices about when to retransmit a packet. Furthermore, in the presence of multiple losses from a single window, NewReno can avoid the multiple halvings of the congestion window that occurred in prior versions.

The details of NewReno are extensive, but the intuition is as follows. If a single packet is lost, then after three duplicate ACKs, the sender will retransmit the lost packet. When it arrives, the receiver will acknowledge all the outstanding data, as it has now filled the one hole in its receive buffer. Conversely, if multiple packets were lost, the first ACK after that retransmitted packet is received will only partially cover the outstanding packets. From this, the sender can infer that

Further Reading:
J. Hoe. Improving the start-up behavior of a congestion control scheme for TCP. SIG-COMM '96. August 1996.

there were more packets lost, and immediately start to try to fill the gaps by sending the next packet that has not yet been acknowledged. This can lead to fewer timeouts and hence less idle time and fewer reductions in the congestion window.

It's worth noting that NewReno was documented in three RFCs published between 1999 and 2012, each one of which fixed some issues in its predecessor's algorithms. This is a case study in how complex it can be to understand the fine detail of congestion control (especially with respect to the subtleties of TCP's retransmission mechanism), adding to the challenge of getting new algorithms into deployment.

4.6 TCP CUBIC

It should be clear by now that trying to find the appropriate rate at which to send traffic into the network is at the heart of congestion control, and that it's possible to err in either direction. Send too little traffic and the network is underutilized leading to poor application performance. Send too much and the network becomes congested, leading to congestion collapse in the worst case. Between these two failure modes, sending too much traffic is generally the more serious, because of the way congestion can quickly compound itself as lost packets are retransmitted. The AIMD approach that is built into Tahoe, Reno and NewReno reflects this: increase the window slowly (additive increase) and decrease it quickly (multiplicative decrease) in an effort to step back from the brink of congestion collapse before it gets too severe. But in high bandwidth-delay environments, the cost of being too conservative in probing for congestion is quite high, as it can take many RTTs before the "pipe is full". So this has led to some rethinking on how to probe for the appropriate window size.

This idea that the window should open quickly at some times and more slowly at others was captured in a new approach called *Binary Increase Congestion Control (BIC)*. Rather than abruptly switching from exponential window growth to linear, as TCP Reno does, BIC effectively does a binary search for the "right" window size. After a packet loss, the congestion window is cut by a multiplicative factor β.

With each successful iteration of sending packets at the new window size, the window is increased to the midpoint of its current value and the old value that caused congestion. In this way, it asymptotes towards the old value—first quickly then slowly. (Taken to the extreme, the window would never get back to its old value—see Zeno's paradox—but when it gets within a certain threshold it is set to the old value).

At this point, if there is no congestion, we can conclude that the network conditions have changed, and it is OK to probe for a new congestion window size. BIC does this first slowly and then more rapidly. You can see the approximate shape of how BIC grows its window in Figure 28, asymptoting towards W_{max} (the old congestion window prior to the last loss) and then moving beyond it.

BIC eventually evolved into a new variant called *CUBIC*, which today is the default congestion control algorithm distributed with Linux. CUBIC improved upon BIC in a number of ways, one of which was to use a smooth curve described by a cubic function rather than the piecewise linear function of BIC. More on this below.

Another important aspect of CUBIC's approach is to adjust its congestion window at regular intervals, based on the amount of time that has elapsed since the last congestion event (e.g., the arrival of a duplicate ACK), rather than only when ACKs arrive (the latter being a function of RTT). This allows CUBIC to behave fairly when long-RTT flows compete with short-RTT flows, which have ACKs arriving more frequently. This is an interesting departure from prior versions of TCP, in which a flow with a short RTT holds a definite advantage in terms of the share of a bottleneck link it will obtain.

The cubic function, shown in Figure 28, has three phases: slowing growth, flatten plateau, increasing growth. The maximum congestion window size achieved just before the last congestion event is the initial target (denoted W_{max}). You can see how the window growth starts fast but slows as you get close to W_{max}; then there is a phase of cautious growth when close to W_{max}, and finally a phase of probing for a new achievable W_{max}.

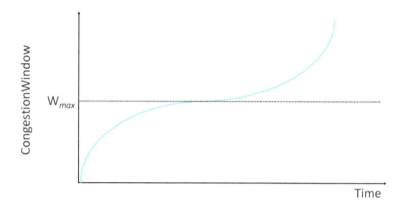

Figure 28: Generic cubic function illustrating the change in the congestion window as a function of time.

Specifically, CUBIC computes the congestion window (CongestionWindow) as a function of time (t) since the last congestion event

$$\text{CongestionWindow}(t) = C \times (t - K)^3 + W_{max}$$

where

$$K = \sqrt[3]{W_{max} \times (1 - \beta)/C}$$

C is a scaling constant and β is the multiplicative decrease factor. CUBIC sets the latter to 0.7 rather than the 0.5 that standard TCP uses. Looking back at Figure 28, CUBIC is often described as shifting between a concave function to being convex (whereas standard TCP's additive function is only convex).

Interestingly, CUBIC is either more aggressive or less aggressive than earlier variants of TCP, depending on the conditions. Short RTT TCP Reno flows tend to be effective in acquiring bottleneck bandwidth, so CUBIC includes a "TCP-friendly" mode where it aims to be just as aggressive as TCP Reno. But in other circumstances—notably high bandwidth-delay networks—CUBIC will be able to obtain a bigger share of the bottleneck bandwidth because CUBIC is increasing its window size more quickly. This brings us back to the discussion of Section 3.3 as to whether "fairness" to incumbent algorithms is the right design goal. Ultimately, CUBIC was extensively analyzed, showed good performance under many conditions without causing undue harm, and has been widely deployed.

Further Reading:
S. Ha, I. Rhee, and L. Xu. CUBIC: a New TCP-friendly High-speed TCP Variant. ACM SIGOPS Operating Systems Review, July 2008.

Chapter 5: Avoidance-Based Algorithms

A review of the academic literature on TCP congestion control shows a notable gap between the original TCP Tahoe and Reno mechanisms introduced in 1988 and 1990, respectively, and the next major flurry of activity starting in 1994, marked by the introduction of an alternative approach known as TCP Vegas. This triggered an avalanche of comparative studies and alternative designs that would persist for the next 25+ years.

Whereas every approach described to date sees packet loss as a congestion signal and tries to react to *control* congestion after the onset, TCP Vegas takes an *avoidance-based* approach to congestion: it tries to detect changes in the measured throughput rate, and adjust the sending rate *before* congestion becomes severe enough to cause packet loss. This chapter describes the general "Vegas strategy", along with three example variations to that strategy introduced over time. This case study culminates in the BBR algorithm championed by Google today.

Further Reading:
L. Brakmo, S. O'Malley and L. Peterson TCP Vegas: New Technique for Congestion Detection and Avoidance. ACM SIGCOMM '94 Symposium. August 1994. (Reprinted in IEEE/ACM Transactions on Networking, October 1995).

5.1 TCP Vegas

The essential idea behind TCP Vegas is to adapt the sending rate based on a comparison of the *measured* throughput rate with the *expected* throughput rate. The intuition can be seen in the trace of TCP Reno given in Figure 29. The top graph traces the connection's congestion window; it shows the same information as the traces given in the previous chapter. The middle and bottom graphs depict new information: the middle graph shows the average sending rate as measured at the source, and the bottom graph shows the average queue length as measured at the bottleneck router. All three graphs are synchronized in time. In the period between 4.5 and 6.0 seconds (shaded region), the congestion window increases (top graph). We expect the observed throughput to also increase, but instead it stays flat (middle graph). This is because the throughput cannot increase beyond the available bandwidth. Beyond this point, any increase in the window size only results in packets taking up buffer space at the bottleneck router (bottom graph).

Figure 29: Congestion window versus observed throughput rate (the three graphs are synchronized). Top, congestion window; middle, observed throughput; bottom, buffer space taken up at the router. Colored line = CongestionWindow; solid bullet = timeout; hash marks = time when each packet is transmitted; vertical bars = time when a packet that was eventually retransmitted was first transmitted.

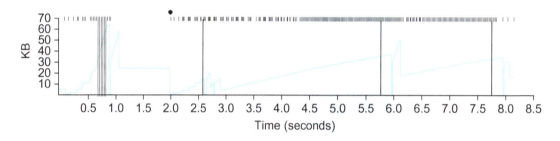

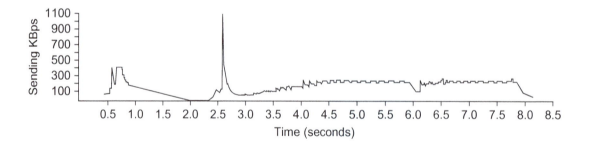

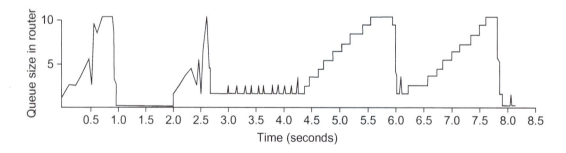

A useful metaphor that describes the phenomenon illustrated in Figure 29 is driving on ice. The speedometer (congestion window) may say that you are going 30 miles an hour, but by looking out the car window and seeing people pass you on foot (measured through-put rate) you know that you are going no more than 5 miles an hour. The uselessly spinning wheels in this analogy are like the extra packets being sent only to sit uselessly in router buffers.

TCP Vegas uses this idea to measure and control the amount of extra data this connection has in transit, where by "extra data" we mean data that the source would not have transmitted had it been able to match exactly the available bandwidth of the network. The goal of TCP Vegas is to maintain the "right" amount of extra data in the network. Obviously, if a source is sending too much extra data, it will cause long delays and possibly lead to congestion. Less obviously, if a connection is sending too little extra data, it cannot respond rapidly enough to transient increases in the available network bandwidth. TCP Vegas's congestion-avoidance actions are based on changes in the estimated amount of extra data in the network, not only on dropped packets. We now describe the algorithm in detail.

First, define a given flow's BaseRTT to be the RTT of a packet when the flow is not congested. In practice, TCP Vegas sets BaseRTT to the minimum of all measured round-trip times; it is commonly the RTT of the first packet sent by the connection, before the router queues increase due to traffic generated by this flow. If we assume that we are not overflowing the connection, then the expected throughput is given by

$$\text{ExpectedRate} = \text{CongestionWindow} / \text{BaseRTT}$$

where CongestionWindow is the TCP congestion window, which we assume (for the purpose of this discussion) to be equal to the number of bytes in transit.

Second, TCP Vegas calculates the current sending rate, ActualRate. This is done by recording the sending time for a distinguished packet, recording how many bytes are transmitted between the time that packet is sent and when its acknowledgment is received, computing the sample RTT for the distinguished packet when its acknowledgment arrives, and dividing the number of bytes transmitted by the sample RTT. This calculation is done once per round-trip time.

Third, TCP Vegas compares ActualRate to ExpectedRate and adjusts the window accordingly. We let Diff = ExpectedRate - ActualRate. Note that Diff is positive or 0 by definition, since the only way ActualRate > ExpectedRate is if the measured sample RTT is less than BaseRTT. If that happens we change BaseRTT to the latest sampled RTT. We also define two thresholds, $\alpha < \beta$, corresponding to having too little and too much extra data in the network, respectively. When Diff < α, TCP Vegas increases the congestion window linearly during the next RTT, and when Diff > β, TCP Vegas decreases the congestion window linearly during the next RTT. TCP Vegas leaves the congestion window unchanged when $\alpha <$ Diff $< \beta$.

Intuitively, we can see that the farther away the actual throughput gets from the expected throughput, the more congestion there is in the network, which implies that the sending rate should be reduced. The β threshold triggers this decrease. On the other hand, when the actual throughput rate gets too close to the expected throughput, the connection is in danger of not utilizing the available bandwidth. The α threshold triggers this increase. The overall goal is to keep between α and β extra bytes in the network.

Figure 30 traces the TCP Vegas congestion-avoidance algorithm. The top graph traces the congestion window, showing the same information as the other traces given throughout this chapter. The bottom graph traces the expected and actual throughput rates that govern how the congestion window is set. It is this bottom graph that best illustrates how the algorithm works. The colored line tracks the ExpectedRate, while the black line tracks the ActualRate. The wide shaded strip gives the region between the α and β thresholds; the top of the shaded strip is α KBps away from ExpectedRate, and the bottom of the shaded strip is β KBps away from ExpectedRate. The goal is to keep the ActualRate between these two thresholds, within the shaded region. Whenever ActualRate falls below the shaded region (i.e., gets too far from ExpectedRate), TCP Vegas decreases the congestion window because it fears that too many packets are being buffered in the network. Likewise, whenever ActualRate goes above the shaded region (i.e., gets

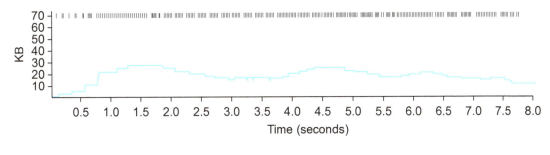

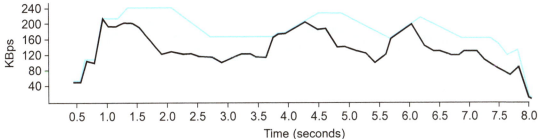

Figure 30: Trace of TCP Vegas congestion-avoidance mechanism. Top, congestion window; bottom, expected (colored line) and actual (black line) throughput. The shaded area is the region between the α and β thresholds.

too close to the ExpectedRate), TCP Vegas increases the congestion window because it fears that it is underutilizing the network.

Because the algorithm, as just presented, compares the difference between the actual and expected throughput rates to the α and β thresholds, these two thresholds are defined in terms of KBps. However, it is perhaps more accurate to think in terms of how many extra *packet buffers* the connection is occupying in the network. For example, on a connection with a BaseRTT of 100 ms and a packet size of 1 KB, if α = 30 KBps and β = 60 KBps, then we can think of α as specifying that the connection needs to be occupying at least 3 extra buffers in the network and β as specifying that the connection should occupy no more than 6 extra buffers in the network. This setting of α and β worked well in practice when Vegas was first deployed, but as we'll see in the next section, these parameters continue to be tuned for changing circumstances.

Finally, you will notice that TCP Vegas decreases the congestion window linearly, seemingly in conflict with the rule that multiplicative decrease is needed to ensure stability. The explanation is that TCP

Vegas does use multiplicative decrease when a timeout occurs; the linear decrease just described is an *early* decrease in the congestion window that should happen before congestion occurs and packets start being dropped.

5.2 Varied Assumptions

TCP Vegas—and Vegas-like approaches to avoiding congestion—have been adapted over time, often in response to different assumptions about the network. Vegas was never as widely deployed as Reno, so the modifications were often driven more by lab studies than extensive real-world experience, but they have collectively refined and contributed to our understanding of avoidance-based algorithms. We summarize some of those insights here, but return to the general topic of customizing the congestion control algorithm for specific use cases in Chapter 7.

5.2.1 FAST TCP

The first Vegas-inspired mechanism was FAST TCP, which was designed to be more efficient on high-speed networks with large bandwidth-delay products. The idea was to increase the congestion window more aggressively during the phase when the algorithm is trying to find the available "in transit" bandwidth (before packets are buffered in the network), and then more conservatively as the algorithm starts to compete with other flows for buffers at the bottleneck router. FAST also recommended adjusting the value of α to roughly 30 packets.

Beyond managing congestion in networks with large bandwidth-delay products, where keeping the pipe full is a substantial challenge, there are two other items of note about FAST. First, whereas both TCP Reno and TCP Vegas were the result of a little intuition and a lot of trial-and-error, FAST was grounded in optimization theory (which was subsequently used to explain why Vegas works). Second, unlike all other congestion control algorithms of which we are aware, an implementation of FAST was made available only as a proprietary solution.

Further Reading:
S. Low, L. Peterson, and L. Wang. Understanding TCP Vegas: A Duality Model.. Journal of the ACM, Volume 49, Issue 2, March 2002.

5.2.2 TCP Westwood

While Vegas was motivated by the idea that congestion can be detected and averted *before* a loss occurs, TCP Westwood (TCPW) is motivated primarily by the realization that packet loss is not always a reliable indicator of congestion. This is particularly noticeable with wireless links, which were a novelty at the time of Vegas but becoming common by the time of TCPW. Wireless links often lose packets due to uncorrected errors on the wireless channel, which are unrelated to congestion. Hence, congestion needs to be detected another way. Interestingly, the end result is somewhat similar to Vegas, in that TCPW also tries to determine the bottleneck bandwidth by looking at the rate at which ACKs are coming back for those packets that were delivered successfully.

When a packet loss occurs, TCPW does not immediately cut the congestion window in half, as it does not yet know if the loss was due to congestion or a link-related packet loss. So instead it estimates the rate at which traffic was flowing right before the packet loss occurred. This is a less aggressive form of backoff than TCP Reno. If the loss was congestion-related, TCPW should send at the rate that was acceptable before the loss. And if the loss was caused by a wireless error, TCPW has not backed off so much, and will start to ramp up again to fully utilize the network. The result was a protocol which performed similarly to Reno for fixed links but outperformed it by substantial margins when lossy links were involved.

Tuning the congestion control algorithm to deal with wireless links continues to be a challenging problem, and to complicate matters, WiFi and the Mobile Cellular network have different properties. We return to this issue in Chapter 7.

5.2.3 New Vegas

Our final example is New Vegas (NV), an adaptation of Vegas's delay-based approach to datacenters, where link bandwidths are 10Gbps or higher and RTTs are typically measured in the tens of microseconds. This is an important use case that we return to in Chapter 7; our goal here is to build some intuition.

To understand the basic idea of NV, suppose that we plot Rate versus CongestionWindow for every packet for which an ACK is received. For the purpose of this exercise, Rate is simply the ratio of CongestionWindow (in bytes) to the RTT of packets that have been ACKed (in seconds). Note that we use CongestionWindow in this discussion for simplicity, while in practice NV uses in-flight (unacknowledged) bytes. When plotted over time, as shown in Figure 31, we end up with vertical bars (rather than points) for values of CongestionWindow due to transient congestion or noise in the measurements.

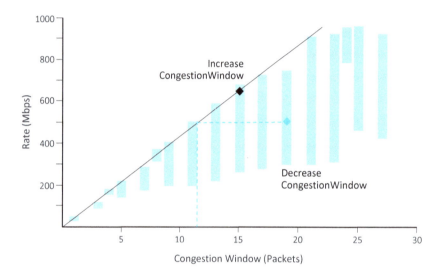

Figure 31: Plotting measured rate vs congestion window.

The maximum slope of the top of the bars indicates the best we have been able to do in the past. In a well tuned system, the top of the bars is bounded by a straight line going through the origin. The idea is that as long as the network is not congested, doubling the amount of data we send per RTT should double the rate.

New measurements of Rate and CongestionWindow can either fall close to the boundary line (black diamond in the figure) or below (blue diamond in the figure). A measurement above the line causes NV to automatically update the line by increasing its slope so the measurement will fall on the new line. If the new measurement is close to the line, then NV increases CongestionWindow. If the measurement is below the line, it means that we have seen equal performance in the past with a lower CongestionWindow. In the example shown in Figure 31, we see similar performance with CongestionWindow=12, so we decrease CongestionWindow. The decrease is done multiplicatively, rather than instantaneously, in case the new measurement is noisy. To filter out bad measurements, NV collects many measurements and then use the best one before making a congestion determination.

5.3 TCP BBR

BBR (Bottleneck Bandwidth and RTT) is a new TCP congestion control algorithm developed by researchers at Google. Like Vegas, BBR is delay based, which means it tries to detect buffer growth so as to avoid congestion and packet loss. Both BBR and Vegas use the minimum RTT and the observed bottleneck bandwidth, as calculated over some time interval, as their main control signals.

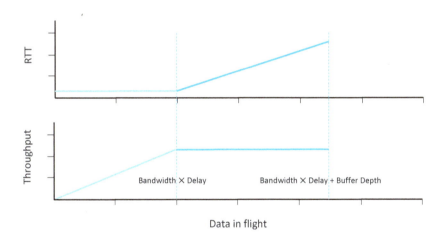

Figure 32: Determining the optimal sending rate based on observed throughput and RTT.

Figure 32 shows the basic idea underlying BBR. Assume a network has a single bottleneck link with some available bandwidth and queuing capacity. As the congestion window opens and more data is put in flight, initially there is an increase in throughput (on the lower graph) but no increase in delay as the bottleneck is not full. Then once the data rate reaches the bottleneck bandwidth, a queue starts to build. At this point, RTT rises, and no rise in throughput is observed. This is the beginning of the congestion phase. This graph is really a simplified version of what we see in the 4.5 to 6.0 second timeframe in Figure 29.

Like Vegas, BBR aims to accurately determine that point where the queue has just started to build, as opposed to continuing all the way to the point of filling the buffer and causing packet drops as Reno does. A lot of the work in BBR has been around improving the sensitivity of the mechanisms that locate that sweet spot. There are numerous challenges: measurements of bandwidth and delay are noisy; network conditions are not static; and the perennial quest for fairness when competing for bandwidth against both BBR and non-BBR flows.

One striking feature of BBR compared to the other approaches we have seen is that it does not rely solely on CongestionWindow to determine how much data is put in flight. Notably, BBR also tries to smooth out the rate at which a sender puts data into the network in an effort to avoid bursts that would lead to excessive queuing. Under ideal conditions, we would like to send data exactly at the rate of the bottleneck, thus achieving the highest possible throughput without causing a queue to build up. Whereas most TCP variants use the arrival of an ACK to "clock" the sending of data, thus ensuring that the amount of unacknowledged data in flight remains constant, BBR creates an estimate of the bottleneck bandwidth and uses a local scheduling algorithm to send data at that rate. ACKs still play an important role in updating knowledge about the state of the network, but they are not directly used to pace transmissions. This means that delayed ACKs do not lead to sudden bursts of transmission. Of course, CongestionWindow is still used to ensure that enough data is sent to keep the pipe full, and to ensure that the amount of data in flight is not so much greater than the bandwidth-delay product as to cause queues to overflow.

In order to maintain an up-to-date view of the current RTT and bottleneck bandwidth, it is necessary to keep probing above and below the current estimate of the bottleneck bandwidth. More bandwidth can become available due to a reduction in the traffic from competing flows, changes in link properties (e.g. on wireless links), or routing changes. Changes in RTT are also possible, particularly if the path changes. To detect a change in RTT it is necessary to send less traffic, hence draining queues. To detect a change in available bandwidth, it is necessary to send more traffic. Hence, BBR probes both above and below its current estimate of the bottleneck bandwidth. If necessary, the estimates are updated, and the sending rate and CongestionWindow are updated accordingly.

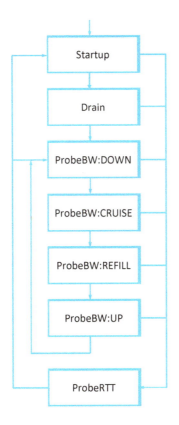

Figure 33: State machine diagram for BBR.

The process of sequentially probing for the available bandwidth and the minimum RTT is captured in the state diagram of Figure 33. After an aggressive startup phase to try to establish the available bandwidth on the path, the sending rate is reduced to drain the queue, and then the algorithm settles into the inner loop of the diagram, in which it periodically checks for better delay at lower sending rates, or better throughput at higher sending rates. On a relatively long timescale (multiple seconds) the algorithm moves into the ProbeRTT state, lowering its sending rate by a factor of two in an effort to fully drain the queue and test for lower RTT.

One interesting aspect of this approach is that when a large flow reduces its sending rate dramatically in the ProbeRTT state, that flow's contribution to queuing delay drops, which causes other flows to simultaneously see a new, lower RTT, and update their estimates. Hence flows show a tendency to synchronize their RTT estimation at times when the queue is actually empty or close to it, improving the accuracy of this estimate.

BBR is actively being worked on and rapidly evolving, with version 2 in use at the time of writing. One major focus is fairness. For example, some early experiments showed CUBIC flows getting 100x less bandwidth when competing with BBR flows, and other experiments show that unfairness among BBR flows is possible. BBR version 1 was insensitive to loss, which could lead to high loss rates particularly when the amount of buffering on the path was relatively low. As several implementations of BBR are now being tried in different environments, including within Google's internal backbone and in the broader Internet, experience is being gathered to further refine the design. The IETF's Congestion Control Working Group is hosting discussions on the ongoing design and experimentation.

Further Reading:
N. Cardwell, Y. Cheng, C. S. Gunn, S. Yeganeh, V. Jacobson. BBR: Congestion-based Congestion Control. Communications of the ACM, Volume 60, Issue 2, February 2017.

Chapter 6: Active Queue Management

We now look at the role routers can play in congestion control, an approach often referred to as *Active Queue Management* (AQM). By its very nature, AQM introduces an element of avoidance to the end-to-end solution, even when paired with a control-based approach like TCP Reno.

Changing router behavior has never been the Internet's preferred way of introducing new features, but nonetheless, the approach has been a constant source of consternation over the last 30 years. The problem is that while it's generally agreed that routers are in an ideal position to detect the onset of congestion—it's their queues that start to fill up—there has not been a consensus on exactly what the best algorithm is. The following describes two of the classic mechanisms, and concludes with a brief discussion of where things stand today.

6.1 DECbit

The first mechanism was developed for use on the Digital Network Architecture (DNA), an early peer of the TCP/IP Internet that also adopted a connectionless/best-effort network model. A description of the approach, published by K.K. Ramakrishnan and Raj Jain, was presented at the same SIGCOMM as the Jacobson/Karels paper in 1988.

The idea is to more evenly split the responsibility for congestion control between the routers and the end hosts. Each router monitors the load it is experiencing and explicitly notifies the end nodes when congestion is about to occur. This notification is implemented

Further Reading:
K.K. Ramakrishnan and R. Jain. A Binary Feedback Scheme for Congestion Avoidance in Computer Networks with a Connectionless Network Layer. ACM SIGCOMM, August 1988.

by setting a binary congestion bit in the packets that flow through the router, which came to be known as the *DECbit*. The destination host then copies this congestion bit into the ACK it sends back to the source. Finally, the source adjusts its sending rate so as to avoid congestion. The following discussion describes the algorithm in more detail, starting with what happens in the router.

A single congestion bit is added to the packet header. A router sets this bit in a packet if its average queue length is greater than or equal to 1 at the time the packet arrives. This average queue length is measured over a time interval that spans the last busy+idle cycle, plus the current busy cycle. (The router is *busy* when it is transmitting and *idle* when it is not.) Figure 34 shows the queue length at a router as a function of time. Essentially, the router calculates the area under the curve and divides this value by the time interval to compute the average queue length. Using a queue length of 1 as the trigger for setting the congestion bit is a trade-off between significant queuing (and hence higher throughput) and increased idle time (and hence lower delay). In other words, a queue length of 1 seems to optimize the power function.

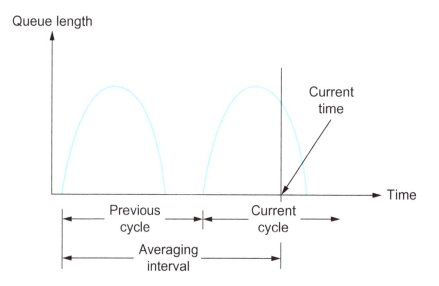

Figure 34: Computing average queue length at a router.

Now turning our attention to the host half of the mechanism, the source records how many of its packets resulted in some router setting the congestion bit. In particular, the source maintains a congestion window, just as in TCP, and watches to see what fraction of the last window's worth of packets resulted in the bit being set. If less than 50% of the packets had the bit set, then the source increases its congestion window by one packet. If 50% or more of the last window's worth of packets had the congestion bit set, then the source decreases its congestion window to 0.875 times the previous value. The value 50% was chosen as the threshold based on analysis that showed it to correspond to the peak of the power curve. The "increase by 1, decrease by 0.875" rule was selected because additive increase/multiplicative decrease makes the mechanism stable.

6.2 Random Early Detection

A second mechanism, called *random early detection* (RED), is similar to the DECbit scheme in that each router is programmed to monitor its own queue length and, when it detects that congestion is imminent, to notify the source to adjust its congestion window. RED, invented by Sally Floyd and Van Jacobson in the early 1990s, differs from the DECbit scheme in two major ways.

The first is that rather than explicitly sending a congestion notification message to the source, RED is most commonly implemented such that it *implicitly* notifies the source of congestion by dropping one of its packets. The source is, therefore, effectively notified by the subsequent timeout or duplicate ACK. As the "early" part of the RED acronym suggests, the gateway drops the packet earlier than it would have to, so as to notify the source that it should decrease its congestion window sooner than it would normally have. In other words, the router drops a few packets before it has exhausted its buffer space completely, so as to cause the source to slow down, with the hope that this will mean it does not have to drop lots of packets later on.

The second difference between RED and DECbit is in the details of how RED decides when to drop a packet and what packet it decides to drop. To understand the basic idea, consider a simple FIFO queue.

Further Reading:
S. Floyd and V. Jacobson
Random Early Detection (RED) Gateways for Congestion Avoidance. IEEE/ACM Transactions on Networking. August 1993.

Rather than wait for the queue to become completely full and then be forced to drop each arriving packet (the tail drop policy described in Section 2.1.3), we could decide to drop each arriving packet with some *drop probability* whenever the queue length exceeds some *drop level*. This idea is called *early random drop*. The RED algorithm defines the details of how to monitor the queue length and when to drop a packet.

In the following paragraphs, we describe the RED algorithm as originally proposed by Floyd and Jacobson. We note that several modifications have since been proposed both by the inventors and by other researchers. However, the key ideas are the same as those presented below, and most current implementations are close to the algorithm that follows.

First, RED computes an average queue length using a weighted running average similar to the one used in the original TCP timeout computation. That is, AvgLen is computed as

$$\text{AvgLen} = (1 - \text{Weight}) \times \text{AvgLen} + \text{Weight} \times \text{SampleLen}$$

where $0 < \text{Weight} < 1$ and SampleLen is the length of the queue when a sample measurement is made. In most software implementations, the queue length is measured every time a new packet arrives at the gateway. In hardware, it might be calculated at some fixed sampling interval.

The reason for using an average queue length rather than an instantaneous one is that it more accurately captures the notion of congestion. Because of the bursty nature of Internet traffic, queues can become full very quickly and then become empty again. If a queue is spending most of its time empty, then it's probably not appropriate to conclude that the router is congested and to tell the hosts to slow down. Thus, the weighted running average calculation tries to detect long-lived congestion, as indicated in the right-hand portion of Figure 35, by filtering out short-term changes in the queue length. You can think of the running average as a low-pass filter, where Weight determines the time constant of the filter. The question of how we pick this time constant is discussed below.

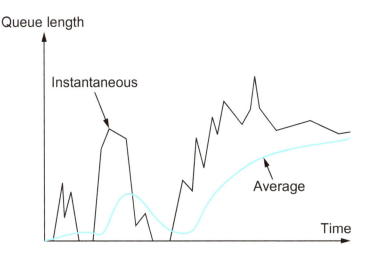

Figure 35: Weighted running average queue length.

Second, RED has two queue length thresholds that trigger certain activity: MinThreshold and MaxThreshold. When a packet arrives at the gateway, RED compares the current AvgLen with these two thresholds, according to the following rules:

```
if AvgLen <= MinThreshold
    queue the packet
if MinThreshold < AvgLen < MaxThreshold
    calculate probability P
    drop the arriving packet with probability P
if MaxThreshold <= AvgLen
    drop the arriving packet
```

If the average queue length is smaller than the lower threshold, no action is taken, and if the average queue length is larger than the upper threshold, then the packet is always dropped. If the average queue length is between the two thresholds, then the newly arriving packet is dropped with some probability P. This situation is depicted in Figure 36. The approximate relationship between P and AvgLen is shown in Figure 37. Note that the probability of drop increases slowly when AvgLen is between the two thresholds, reaching MaxP at the upper threshold, at which point it jumps to unity. The rationale behind this is that, if AvgLen reaches the upper threshold, then the gentle approach (dropping a few packets) is not working and drastic measures are called for: dropping all arriving packets. Some research has suggested that a smoother transition from random dropping to complete dropping, rather than the discontinuous approach shown here, may be appropriate.

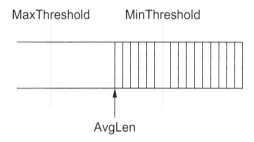

Figure 36: RED thresholds on a FIFO queue.

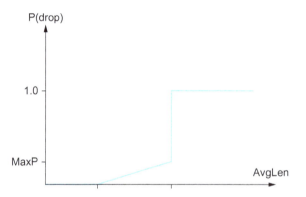

Figure 37: Drop probability function for RED.

Although Figure 37 shows the probability of drop as a function only of AvgLen, the situation is actually a little more complicated. In fact, P is a function of both AvgLen and how long it has been since the last packet was dropped. Specifically, it is computed as follows:

$$\text{TempP} = \text{MaxP} \times (\text{AvgLen} - \text{MinThreshold}) \,/\, (\text{MaxThreshold} - \text{MinThreshold})$$

$$P = \text{TempP} \,/\, (1 - \text{count} \times \text{TempP})$$

TempP is the variable that is plotted on the y-axis in Figure 37, count keeps track of how many newly arriving packets have been queued (not dropped), and AvgLen has been between the two thresholds. P increases slowly as count increases, thereby making a drop increasingly likely as the time since the last drop increases. This makes closely spaced drops relatively less likely than widely spaced drops. This extra step in calculating P was introduced by the inventors of RED when they observed that, without it, the packet drops were not well distributed in time but instead tended to occur in clusters. Because packet arrivals from a certain connection are likely to arrive in bursts, this clustering of drops is likely to cause multiple drops in a single connection. This is not desirable, since only one drop per round-trip time is enough to cause a connection to reduce its window size, whereas multiple drops might send it back into slow start.

As an example, suppose that we set MaxP to 0.02 and count is initialized to zero. If the average queue length were halfway between the two thresholds, then TempP, and the initial value of P, would be half of MaxP, or 0.01. An arriving packet, of course, has a 99 in 100 chance of getting into the queue at this point. With each successive packet that is not dropped, P slowly increases, and by the time 50 packets have arrived without a drop, P would have doubled to 0.02. In the unlikely event that 99 packets arrived without loss, P reaches 1, guaranteeing that the next packet is dropped. This part of the algorithm ensures a roughly even distribution of drops over time.

The intent is that, if RED drops a small percentage of packets when AvgLen exceeds MinThreshold, this will cause a few TCP connections to reduce their window sizes, which in turn will reduce the rate at which packets arrive at the router. All going well, AvgLen will then decrease and congestion is avoided. The queue length can be kept short, while throughput remains high since few packets are dropped.

Note that, because RED is operating on a queue length averaged over time, it is possible for the instantaneous queue length to be much longer than AvgLen. In this case, if a packet arrives and there is nowhere to put it, then it will have to be dropped. When this happens, RED is operating in tail drop mode. One of the goals of RED is to prevent tail drop behavior if possible.

The random nature of RED confers an interesting property on the algorithm. Because RED drops packets randomly, the probability that

RED decides to drop a particular flow's packet(s) is roughly proportional to the share of the bandwidth that flow is currently getting at that router. This is because a flow that is sending a relatively large number of packets is providing more candidates for random dropping. Thus, there is some sense of fair resource allocation built into RED, although it is by no means precise. While arguably fair, because RED punishes high-bandwidth flows more than low-bandwidth flows, it increases the probability of a TCP restart, which is doubly painful for those high-bandwidth flows.

A fair amount of analysis has gone into setting the various RED parameters—for example, MaxThreshold, MinThreshold, MaxP and Weight—all in the name of optimizing the power function (throughput-to-delay ratio). The performance of these parameters has also been confirmed through simulation, and the algorithm has been shown not to be overly sensitive to them. It is important to keep in mind, however, that all of this analysis and simulation hinges on a particular characterization of the network workload. The real contribution of RED is a mechanism by which the router can more accurately manage its queue length. Defining precisely what constitutes an optimal queue length depends on the traffic mix and is a subject of ongoing study.

Consider the setting of the two thresholds, MinThreshold and MaxThreshold. If the traffic is fairly bursty, then MinThreshold should be sufficiently large to allow the link utilization to be maintained at an acceptably high level. Also, the difference between the two thresholds should be larger than the typical increase in the calculated average queue length in one RTT. Setting MaxThreshold to twice MinThreshold seems to be a reasonable rule of thumb given the traffic mix on today's Internet. In addition, since we expect the average queue length to hover between the two thresholds during periods of high load, there should be enough free buffer space *above* MaxThreshold to absorb the natural bursts that occur in Internet traffic without forcing the router to enter tail drop mode.

We noted above that Weight determines the time constant for the running average low-pass filter, and this gives us a clue as to how we might pick a suitable value for it. Recall that RED is trying to send signals to TCP flows by dropping packets during times of congestion.

Suppose that a router drops a packet from some TCP connection and then immediately forwards some more packets from the same connection. When those packets arrive at the receiver, it starts sending duplicate ACKs to the sender. When the sender sees enough duplicate ACKs, it will reduce its window size. So, from the time the router drops a packet until the time when the same router starts to see some relief from the affected connection in terms of a reduced window size, at least one round-trip time must elapse for that connection. There is probably not much point in having the router respond to congestion on time scales much less than the round-trip time of the connections passing through it. As noted previously, 100 ms is not a bad estimate of average round-trip times in the Internet. Thus, Weight should be chosen such that changes in queue length over time scales much less than 100 ms are filtered out.

Since RED works by sending signals to TCP flows to tell them to slow down, you might wonder what would happen if those signals are ignored. This is often called the *unresponsive flow* problem. Unresponsive flows use more than their fair share of network resources and could cause congestive collapse if there were enough of them, just as in the days before TCP congestion control. Some queueing techniques, such as weighted fair queueing, could help with this problem by isolating certain classes of traffic from others. There was also discussion of creating a variant of RED that could drop more heavily from flows that are unresponsive to the initial hints that it sends. However this turns out to be challenging because it can be hard to distinguish between non-responsive behavior and "correct" behavior, especially when flows have a wide variety of different RTTs and bottleneck bandwidths.

As a footnote, 15 prominent network researchers urged for the widespread adoption of RED-inspired AQM in 1998. The recommendation was largely ignored, for reasons that we touch on below. AQM approaches based on RED have, however, been applied with some success in datacenters.

Further Reading:
R. Braden, *et al.* Recommendations on Queue Management and Congestion Avoidance in the Internet. RFC 2309, April 1998.

6.3 Controlled Delay

As noted in the preceding section, RED has never been widely adopted. Certainly it never reached the level necessary to have a significant impact on congestion in the Internet. One reason is that RED is difficult to configure in a way that consistently improves performance. Note the large number of parameters that affect its operation (MinThreshold, MaxThreshold, and Weight). There is enough research showing that RED produces a wide range of outcomes (not all of them helpful) depending on the type of traffic and parameter settings. This created uncertainty around the merits of deploying it.

Over a period of years, Van Jacobson (well known for his work on TCP Congestion and a co-author of the original RED paper) collaborated with Kathy Nichols and eventually other researchers to come up with an AQM approach that improves upon RED. This work became known as CoDel (pronounced *coddle*) for Controlled Delay AQM. CoDel builds on several key insights that emerged over decades of experience with TCP and AQM.

First, queues are an important aspect of networking and it is expected that queues will build up from time to time. For example, a newly opened connection may dump a window's worth of packets into the network, and these are likely to form a queue at the bottleneck link. This is not in itself a problem. There should be enough buffer capacity to absorb such bursts. Problems arise when there is not enough buffer capacity to absorb bursts, leading to excessive loss. This came to be understood in the 1990s as a requirement that buffers be able to hold at least one bandwidth-delay product of packets—a requirement that was probably too large and subsequently questioned by further research. But the fact is that buffers are necessary, and it is expected that they will be used to absorb bursts. The CoDel authors refer to this as "good queue", as illustrated in Figure 38 (a).

Queues become a problem when they are persistently full. A persistently full queue is doing nothing except adding delay to the network, and it is also less able to absorb bursts if it never drains fully. The combination of large buffers and persistent queues within those buffers is a phenomenon that Jim Gettys has named *Bufferbloat*. It

Further Reading:
K. Nichols and V. Jacobson. Controlling Queue Delay. ACM Queue, 10(5), May 2012.

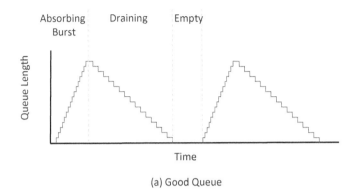

(a) Good Queue

Figure 38: Good and Bad Queue Scenarios

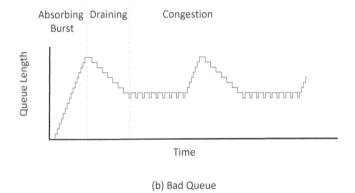

(b) Bad Queue

is clear that persistently full queues are what a well-designed AQM mechanism would seek to avoid. Queues that stay full for long periods without draining are referred to, unsurprisingly, as "bad queue", as shown in Figure 38 (b).

In a sense, then, the challenge for an AQM algorithm is to distinguish between "good" and "bad" queues, and to trigger packet loss only when the queue is determined to be "bad". Indeed, this is what RED is trying to do with its weight parameter (which filters out transient queue length).

One of the innovations of CoDel is to focus on *sojourn time*: the time that any given packet waits in the queue. Sojourn time is independent of the bandwidth of a link and provides useful indication of conges-

Further Reading:
J. Gettys. Bufferbloat: Dark Buffers in the Internet. IEEE Internet Computing, April 2011.

tion even on links whose bandwidth varies over time, such as wireless links. A queue that is behaving well will frequently drain to zero, and thus, some packets will experience a sojourn time close to zero, as in Figure 38 (a). Conversely, a congested queue will delay every packet, and the minimum sojourn time will never be close to zero, as seen in Figure 38 (b). CoDel therefore measures the sojourn time—something that is easy to do for every packet—and tracks whether it is consistently sitting above some small target. "Consistently" is defined as "lasting longer than a typical RTT".

Rather than asking operators to determine the parameters to make CoDel work well, the algorithm chooses reasonable defaults. A target sojourn time of 5ms is used, along with a sliding measurement window of 100ms. The intuition, as with RED, is that 100ms is a typical RTT for traffic traversing the Internet, and that if congestion is lasting longer than 100ms, we may be moving into the "bad queue" region. So CoDel monitors the sojourn time relative to the target of 5ms. If it is above target for more than 100ms, it is time to start taking action to reduce the queue via drops (or marking if explicit congestion notification, described below, is available). 5ms is chosen as being close to zero (for better delay) but not so small that the queue would run empty. It should be noted that a great deal of experimentation and simulation has gone into these numerical choices, but more importantly, the algorithm does not seem to be overly sensitive to them.

To summarize, CoDel largely ignore queues that last less than an RTT, but starts taking action as soon as a queue persists for more than an RTT. By making reasonable assumptions about Internet RTTs, the algorithm requires no configuration parameters.

An additional subtlety is that CoDel drops a slowly increasing percentage of traffic as long as the observed sojourn time remains above the target. As discussed further in Section 7.4, TCP throughput has been shown to depend inversely on the square root of loss rate. Thus, as long as the sojourn time stays above the target, CoDel steadily increases its drop rate in proportion to the square root of the number of drops since the target was exceeded. The effect of this, in theory, is to cause a linear decrease in throughput of the affected TCP connections. Eventually this should lead to enough reduction in arriving traffic to allow the queue to drain, bringing the sojourn time back below the target.

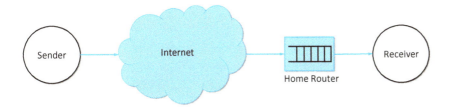

Figure 39: Home routers can suffer from bufferbloat, a situation CoDel is well-suited to address.

There are more details to CoDel presented in the Nichols and Jacobson paper, including extensive simulations to indicate its effectiveness across a wide range of scenarios. The algorithm has been standardized as "experimental" by the IETF in RFC 8289. It is also implemented in the Linux kernel, which has aided in its deployment. In particular, CoDel provides value in home routers (which are often Linux-based), a point along the end-to-end path (see Figure 39) that commonly experiences bufferbloat.

6.4 Explicit Congestion Notification

While TCP's congestion control mechanism was initially based on packet loss as the primary congestion signal, it has long been recognized that TCP could do a better job if routers were to send a more explicit congestion signal. That is, instead of *dropping* a packet and assuming TCP will eventually notice (e.g., due to the arrival of a duplicate ACK), any AQM algorithm can potentially do a better job if it instead *marks* the packet and continues to send it along its way to the destination. This idea was codified in changes to the IP and TCP headers known as *Explicit Congestion Notification* (ECN), as specified in RFC 3168.

Specifically, this feedback is implemented by treating two bits in the IP TOS field as ECN bits. One bit is set by the source to indicate that it is ECN-capable, that is, able to react to a congestion notification. This is called the ECT bit (ECN-Capable Transport). The other bit is set by routers along the end-to-end path when congestion is encountered,

Further Reading:
K. Ramakrishnan, S. Floyd, and D. Black. The Addition of Explicit Congestion Notification (ECN) to IP. RFC 3168, September 2001.

as computed by whatever AQM algorithm it is running. This is called the CE bit (Congestion Encountered).

In addition to these two bits in the IP header (which are transport-agnostic), ECN also includes the addition of two optional flags to the TCP header. The first, ECE (ECN-Echo), communicates from the receiver to the sender that it has received a packet with the CE bit set. The second, CWR (Congestion Window Reduced) communicates from the sender to the receiver that it has reduced the congestion window.

While ECN is now the standard interpretation of two of the eight bits in the TOS field of the IP header and support for ECN is highly recommended, it is not required. Moreover, there is no single recommended AQM algorithm, but instead, there is a list of requirements a good AQM algorithm should meet. Like TCP congestion control algorithms, every AQM algorithm has its advantages and disadvantages, and so we need a lot of them to argue about.

6.5 Ingress/Egress Queues

We have been drawing a clear line between approaches to congestion control that happen *inside the network* (i.e., the AQM algorithms described in this chapter) and *at the edge of the network* (i.e., the TCP-based algorithms described in earlier chapters). But the line isn't necessarily that crisp. To see this, you just have to think of the end-to-end path as having a *ingress queue* at the kernel/device interface on the sending host and an *egress queue* at the device/kernel interface on the receiving host.[3] These edge queues are likely to become increasingly important as virtual switches and NIC support for virtualization become more and more common.

This perspective is illustrated in Figure 40, where both locations sit below TCP, and provide an opportunity to inject a second piece of congestion control logic into the end-to-end path. CoDel and ECN are examples of this idea: they have been implemented at the device queue level of the Linux kernel.

Does this work? One issue is whether packets are dropped at the ingress or the egress. When dropping at the ingress (on the sending host), TCP is notified in the return value of the *Write* function, which

[3] Confusingly, the *ingress queue* from the perspective of the network path is the outbound (egress) queue on the sending host and, the *egress queue* from the perspective of the network path is the inbound (ingress) queue on the receiving host. As shown in Figure 40, we use the terms ingress and egress from the network's perspective.

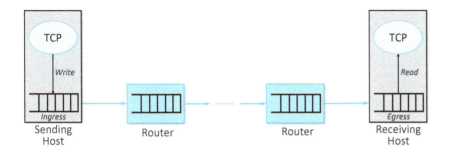

Figure 40: Ingress and egress queues along the end-to-end path, implemented in the sending and receiving hosts, respectively.

causes it to "forget" that it sent the packet. This means this packet will be sent next, although TCP does decrease its congestion window in response to the failed write. In contrast, dropping packets at the egress queue (on the receiving host), means the TCP sender will not know to retransmit the packet until it detects the loss using one of its standard mechanisms (e.g., three duplicate ACKs, a timeout). Of course, having the egress implement ECN helps.

When we consider this discussion in the context of the bigger congestion control picture, we can make two interesting observations. One is that Linux provides a convenient and safe way to inject new code—including congestion control logic—into the kernel, namely, using the *extended Berkeley Packet Filter (eBPF)*. eBPF is becoming an important technology in many other contexts as well. The standard kernel API for congestion control has been ported to eBPF and most existing congestion control algorithms have been ported to this framework. This simplifies the task of experimenting with new algorithms or tweaking existing algorithms by side-stepping the hurdle of waiting for the relevant Linux kernel to be deployed.

A second observation is that by explicitly exposing the ingress/egress queues to the decision-making process, we open the door to building a congestion control mechanism that contains both a "decide when to transmit a packet" component and a "decide to queue-or-drop a packet" component. We'll see an example of a mechanism that takes an innovative approach to using these two components in Section 7.1 when we describe On-Ramp.

Further Reading:
The Linux Kernel. BPF Documentation.

Chapter 7: Beyond TCP

As exploration of the design space for congestion control has continued, a number of new algorithms and protocols have emerged. These differ from what we've seen in earlier chapters mostly in that they target specific use cases, rather than the arbitrarily complex and heterogeneous network environments that TCP supports. The exception may be QUIC, which started with the goal of improving HTTP performance specifically, but has now developed into something of a general TCP alternative.

This chapter is not exhaustive, but we instead survey a few specific use cases. These include tuning TCP performance for datacenters; sending background traffic over an extended period of time using only excess capacity; optimizing HTTP-based web traffic without being backward-compatible with TCP; supporting real-time streaming in a way that is TCP-friendly; supporting multipath transport protocols; and accommodating mobile cellular networks with unique radio-induced behavior.

7.1 Datacenters (DCTCP, On-Ramp)

There have been several efforts to optimize TCP for cloud datacenters, where *Data Center TCP* was one of the first. There are several aspects of the datacenter environment that warrant an approach that differs from more traditional TCP. These include:

- Round trip time for intra-DC traffic are small;

- Buffers in datacenter switches are also typically small;

- All the switches are under common administrative control, and thus can be required to meet certain standards;

- A great deal of traffic has low latency requirements;

- That traffic competes with high bandwidth flows.

It should be noted that DCTCP is not just a version of TCP, but rather, a system design that changes both the switch behavior and the end host response to congestion information received from switches.

The central insight in DCTCP is that using loss as the main signal of congestion in the datacenter environment is insufficient. By the time a queue has built up enough to overflow, low latency traffic is already failing to meet its deadlines, negatively impacting performance. Thus DCTCP uses a version of ECN to provide an early signal of congestion. But whereas the original design of ECN treated an ECN marking much like a dropped packet, and cut the congestion window in half, DCTCP takes a more finely-tuned approach. DCTCP tries to estimate the fraction of bytes that are encountering congestion rather than making the simple binary decision that congestion is present. It then scales the congestion window based on this estimate. The standard TCP algorithm still kicks in should a packet actually be lost. The approach is designed to keep queues short by reacting early to congestion while not over-reacting to the point that they run empty and sacrifice throughput.

The key challenge in this approach is to estimate the fraction of bytes encountering congestion. Each switch is simple. If a packet arrives and the switch sees the queue length (K) is above some threshold; e.g.,

$$K > (RTT \times C) / 7$$

where C is the link rate in packets per second, then the switch sets the CE bit in the IP header. The complexity of RED is not required.

The receiver then maintains a boolean variable for every flow, which we'll denote DCTCP.CE, and sets it initially to false. When sending an ACK, the receiver sets the ECE (Echo Congestion Experienced) flag in the TCP header if and only if DCTCP.CE is true. It also implements the following state machine in response to every received packet:

- If the CE bit is set and DCTCP.CE=False, set DCTCP.CE to True and send an immediate ACK.

- If the CE bit is not set and DCTCP.CE=True, set DCTCP.CE to False and send an immediate ACK.

- Otherwise, ignore the CE bit.

The non-obvious consequence of the "otherwise" case is that the receiver continues to send delayed ACKs once every n packets, as long as a stream of packets with a constant CE value is received. Delayed ACKs have proven important to maintaining high performance.

At the end of each observation window (a period usually chosen to be approximately the RTT), the sender computes the fraction of bytes that encountered congestion during that window as the ratio of the bytes marked with CE to total bytes transmitted. DCTCP grows the congestion window in exactly the same way as the standard algorithm, but it reduces the window in proportion to how many bytes encountered congestion during the last observation window.

Specifically, a new variable called DCTCP.Alpha is initialized to 1 and updated at the end of the observation window as follows:

$$\text{DCTCP.Alpha} = \text{DCTCP.Alpha} \times (1 - g) + g \times M$$

M is the faction of bytes marked, and g is the estimation gain, a constant (set by the implementation) that determines how rapidly DCTCP.Alpha changes in response to marking of packets. When there is sustained congestion, DCTCP.Alpha approaches 1, and when there is sustained lack of congestion, DCTCP.Alpha decays to zero. This causes gentle reaction to newly arrived congestion and more severe reaction to sustained congestion, as the congestion window is calculated as follows:

$$\text{CongestionWindow} = \text{CongestionWindow} \times (1 - \text{DCTCP.Alpha} / 2)$$

To summarize, CE marking to indicate incipient congestion happens early and often, but the reaction to such marking is more measured

120

than in standard TCP, to avoid the over-reaction that would lead to queues running empty.

The paper that lays out all the arguments for DCTCP including a study of the datacenter traffic characteristics that motivated its design is a "test of time" award winner from SIGCOMM.

Further Reading:
M. Alizadeh, *et al.* Data Center TCP (DCTCP). ACM SIG-COMM, August 2010.

There has been considerable research since DCTCP to optimize TCP for datacenters, with the general approach being to introduce ever-more sophisticated signals from the network that the sender can use to manage congestion. We conclude our discussion of this use case by elaborating on one of the most recent efforts, On-Ramp, because it focuses instead on the fundamental tension that all congestion control algorithms face: The trade-off between reaching equilibrium for long-lived flows versus dealing with transient bursts. On-Ramp adopts a modular design that directly addresses this tension, and does so without depending on additional feedback from the network.

The main insight is that when a congestion control algorithm in equilibrium encounters severe congestion and drastically cuts its window (or rate), it must decide whether or not to remember its previous equilibrium state. This is a difficult choice because it depends on the duration of congestion, which is hard to predict. If the congestion is transient, the algorithm should remember its previous state so it can rapidly restore the old equilibrium without under-utilizing the network once the burst ends. If the congestion is sustained, for example due to the arrival of one or more new flows, the algorithm should forget its previous state so that it can rapidly find a new equilibrium.

The idea is to break the congestion control mechanism into two parts, with each focused on just one aspect of the equilibrium/transient trade-off. Specifically, On-Ramp is implemented as a "shim" that sits below a conventional TCP congestion control algorithm, as shown in Figure 41. The On-Ramp shim deals with bursts (which temporarily fill network queues) by trying to quickly reduce queuing delays whenever the measured *One-Way Delay (OWD)* grows too large. It does this by temporarily holding packets at the sender (rather than letting them occupy an in-network buffer) whenever OWD is greater than some threshold. The On-Ramp shim is then composed with an existing congestion control algorithm, which continues to work towards reaching

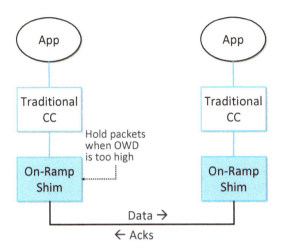

Figure 41: On-Ramp paces packet transmission to avoid in-network queues due to bursty traffic, complementing the traditional congestion control algorithm's effort to maintain long-term stability and fairness.

equilibrium for long-term flows. On-Ramp has been shown to work with several existing congestion control algorithms, including DCTCP.

The key is that On-Ramp is designed so the two control decisions run independently, on their own timescale. But to work, the shim needs to accurately measure OWD, which in turn depends on synchronized clocks between the sender and receiver. Since datacenter delays can be less than a few tens of microseconds, the sender and receiver clocks must be synchronized to within a few microseconds. Such high-accuracy clock synchronization has traditionally required hardware-intensive protocols, but On-Ramp leverages a new approach that takes advantage of the network effect in a mesh of cooperating nodes to achieve nanosecond-level clock synchronization. It does so without special hardware, making On-Ramp easy to deploy.

7.2 Background Transport (LEDBAT)

In sharp contrast to low-latency datacenter environments, there are many applications that need to transfer a large amount of data over an extended period of time. File-sharing protocols such as BitTorrent and software-updates are two examples. LEDBAT (Low Extra Delay Background Transport) is targeted at these applications.

One of the common themes among various efforts to improve

Further Reading:

S. Liu, *et al*. Breaking the Transience-Equilibrium Nexus: A New Approach to Datacenter Packet Transport. Usenix NSDI '21. April 2021.

Y. Geng, *et al*. Exploiting a Natural Network Effect for Scalable, Fine-grained Clock Synchronization. Usenix NSDI '18, April 2018.

TCP's congestion control algorithm has been the idea of co-existence with standard TCP. It is well-known that an algorithm could "outperform" TCP by simply being more aggressive in its response to congestion. Hence, there is an implicit assumption that new congestion control algorithms should be evaluated alongside standard TCP to ensure they are not just stealing bandwidth from less aggressive TCP implementations.

LEDBAT takes this idea in the opposite direction by creating a congestion control protocol that is purposely *less* aggressive than TCP. The idea is to take advantage of bandwidth that is available when links are uncongested, but to quickly back off and leave the bandwidth free for other, standard flows when they arrive. In addition, as the name suggests, LEDBAT tries not to create significant queuing delays, unlike the typical behavior of TCP when filling a bottleneck link.

Like TCP Vegas, LEDBAT aims to detect the onset of congestion before it is severe enough to cause loss. However, LEDBAT takes a different approach to making this determination, using one-way measurements of delay as the primary input to the process. This is a relatively novel approach that makes sense in an era where reasonably accurate but not perfectly synchronized clocks are assumed to be the norm.

To calculate one-way delay, the sender puts a timestamp in each transmitted packet, and the receiver compares this against local system time to measure the delay experienced by the packet. It then sends this calculated value back to the sender. Even though the clocks are not precisely synchronized, *changes* in this delay can be used to infer the buildup of queues. It is assumed that the clocks do not have large relative "skew", i.e., their relative offset does not change too quickly, which is a reasonable assumption in practice.

The sender monitors the measured delay, and estimates the fixed component (which is due to speed of light and other fixed delays) to be the lowest value seen over a certain (configurable) time interval. Estimates from the more distant past are eliminated to allow for the possibility of a new routing path changing the fixed delay. Any delay larger than this minimum is assumed to be due to queuing delay.

Having established a "base" delay, the sender subtracts this from the measured delay to obtain the queuing delay, and optionally uses a filtering algorithm to reduce short-term noise in the estimate. This estimated queuing delay is then compared to a target delay. When the delay is below target, the congestion window is allowed to grow, and when the delay is above target, the congestion window is reduced, with the rate of growth and decrease being proportional to the distance from the target. The growth rate is capped to be no faster than the growth of standard TCP's window in its additive increase phase.

LEDBAT's algorithm for computing how much to increment the CongestionWindow when an ACK is received can be summarized as follows:

$$\text{Increment} = \text{GAIN} \times \text{off\_target} \times \text{newly\_acked} \times \text{MSS}/\text{CongestionWindow}$$

where GAIN is a configuration parameter between 0 and 1, off_target is the gap between the measured queuing delay and the target, expressed as a fraction of the target, and newly_acked is the number of bytes acknowledged in the current ACK. Thus, the congestion window grows more quickly the further the measured delay is below the target, but never faster than one MSS per RTT. And it falls faster in proportion to how far the queue length is above the target. CongestionWindow is also reduced in response to losses, timeouts, and long idle periods, much like with TCP.

Hence, LEDBAT can do a good job of using available bandwidth that is free, but avoids creating long standing queues, as it aims to keep the delay around the target (which is a configurable number, suggested to be on the order of 100 ms). If other traffic starts to compete with LEDBAT traffic, LEDBAT will back off as it aims to prevent the queue getting longer.

LEDBAT is defined as an experimental protocol by the IETF, and allows a considerable degree of implementation flexibility such as the choice of filtering on delay estimates and a range of configuration parameters. Further details can be found in the RFC.

Further Reading:
S. Shalunov, *et al.* Low Extra Delay Background Transport (LEDBAT). RFC 6817, December 2012.

7.3 HTTP Performance (QUIC)

HTTP has been around since the invention of the World Wide Web in the 1990s and from its inception it has run over TCP. HTTP/1.0, the original version, had quite a number of performance problems due to the way it used TCP, such as the fact that every request for an object required a new TCP connection to be set up and then closed after the reply was returned. HTTP/1.1 was proposed at an early stage to make better use of TCP. TCP continued to be the protocol used by HTTP for another twenty-plus years.

In fact, TCP continued to be problematic as a protocol to support the Web, especially because a reliable, ordered byte stream isn't exactly the right model for Web traffic. In particular, since most web pages contain many objects, it makes sense to be able to request many objects in parallel, but TCP only provides a single byte stream. If one packet is lost, TCP waits for its retransmission and successful delivery before continuing, while HTTP would have been happy to receive other objects that were not affected by that single lost packet. Opening multiple TCP connections would appear to be a solution to this, but that has its own set of drawbacks including a lack of shared information about congestion across connections.

Other factors such as the rise of high-latency wireless networks, the availability of multiple networks for a single device (e.g., Wi-Fi and cellular), and the increasing use of encrypted, authenticated connections on the Web also contributed to the realization that the transport layer for HTTP would benefit from a new approach. The protocol that emerged to fill this need was QUIC.

QUIC originated at Google in 2012 and was subsequently developed as a proposed standard at the IETF. It has already seen a solid amount of deployment—it is in most Web browsers, many popular Web sites, and is even starting to be used for non-HTTP applications. Deployability was a key consideration for the designers of the protocol. There are a lot of moving parts to QUIC—its specification spans three RFCs of several hundred pages—but we focus here on its approach to congestion control, which embraces many of the ideas we have seen to date in this book.

Like TCP, QUIC builds congestion control into the transport, but it does so in a way that recognizes that there is no single perfect congestion control algorithm. Instead, there is an assumption that different senders may use different algorithms. The baseline algorithm in the QUIC specification is similar to TCP NewReno, but a sender can unilaterally choose a different algorithm to use, such as CUBIC. QUIC provides all the machinery to detect lost packets in support of various congestion control algorithms.

A number of design features of QUIC make the detection of loss and congestion more robust than in TCP. For example, whereas TCP uses the same sequence number for a packet whether it is being sent for the first time or retransmitted, QUIC sequence numbers (called packet numbers) are strictly increasing. A higher packet number signifies that the packet was sent later, and a lower packet number signifies that the packet was sent earlier. This means that it is always possible to distinguish between a packet that has been transmitted for the first time and one that has been retransmitted due to a loss or timeout.

Note also that whereas TCP sequence numbers refer to bytes in the transmitted byte stream, QUIC packet numbers refer to entire packets. The packet number space for QUIC is large enough to avoid wraparound issues (up to $2^{62} - 1$).

QUIC builds selective acknowledgments into the protocol, with support for more than the three ranges of packets that can be acknowledged in the TCP SACK option. This improves performance in high loss environments, enabling forward progress to be made as long as some packets are getting received successfully.

QUIC adopts a more robust approach to determining packet loss than the duplicate ACKs on which TCP Fast Recovery relies. The approach was developed independent of QUIC under the name RACK-TLP: Recent Acknowledgments and Tail Loss Probes. A key insight is that duplicate ACKs fail to trigger loss recovery when the sender doesn't send enough data after the lost packet to trigger the duplicate ACKs, or when retransmitted packets are themselves lost. Conversely, packet reordering may also trigger fast recovery when in fact no packets have been lost. QUIC takes the ideas of RACK-TLP to address this by using a pair of mechanisms:

- A packet is considered lost if a packet with a higher number has been acknowledged, and the packet was sent "long enough in the past" or K packets before the acknowledged packet (K is a parameter).

- Probe packets are sent after waiting a "probe timeout interval" for an ACK to arrive, in an effort to trigger an ACK that will provide information about lost packets.

The first bullet ensures that modest amounts of packet reordering are not interpreted as loss events. K is recommended to be initially set to 3, but can be updated if there is evidence of greater misordering. And the definition of "long enough in the past" is a little more than the measured RTT.

The second bullet ensures that, even if duplicate ACKs are not generated by data packets, probe packets are sent to elicit further ACKs, thus exposing gaps in the received packet stream. The "probe timeout interval" is calculated to be just long enough to account for all the delays that an ACK might have encountered, using both the estimated RTT and an estimate of its variance.

QUIC is a most interesting development in the world of transport protocols. Many of the limitations of TCP have been known for decades, but QUIC represents one of the most successful efforts to date to stake out a different point in the design space. It has also built in decades worth of experience refining TCP congestion control into the baseline specification. Because QUIC was inspired by experience with HTTP and the Web—which arose long after TCP was well established in the Internet—it presents a fascinating case study in the unforeseen consequences of layered designs and in the evolution of the Internet. There is a lot more to it that we can cover here. The definitive reference for QUIC is RFC 9000, but congestion control is covered in the separate RFC 9002.

Further Reading:
J. Iyengar and I. Swett, Eds. QUIC Loss Detection and Congestion Control. RFC 9002, May 2021.

7.4 TCP-Friendly Protocols (TFRC)

As noted at various points throughout this book, it is easy to make transport protocols that out-perform TCP, since TCP in all its forms backs off when it detects congestion. Any protocol which does *not* respond to congestion with a reduction in sending rate will eventually get a bigger share of the bottleneck link than any TCP or TCP-like traffic that it competes against. In the limit, this would likely lead back to the congestion collapse that was starting to become common when TCP congestion control was first developed. Hence, there is a strong interest in making sure that the vast majority of traffic on the Internet is in some sense "TCP-friendly".

When we use the term "TCP-friendly" we are saying that we expect a similar congestion response to that of TCP. LEDBAT could be considered "more than TCP-friendly" in the sense that it backs off even more aggressively to congestion than TCP by reducing its window size at the first hint of delay. But there is a class of applications for which being TCP-friendly requires a bit more thought because they do not use a window-based congestion scheme. These are typically "real time" applications involving streaming multimedia.

Multimedia applications such as video streaming and telephony can adjust their sending rate by changing coding parameters, with a trade-off between bandwidth and quality. However, they cannot suddenly reduce sending rate by a large amount without a perceptible impact on the quality, and they generally need to choose among a finite set of quality levels. These considerations lead to rate-based approaches rather than window-based, as discussed in Section 3.1.

The approach to TCP-friendliness for these applications is to try to pick a sending rate similar to that which would be achieved by TCP under similar conditions, but to do so in a way that keeps the rate from fluctuating too wildly. Underpinning this idea is a body of research going back many years on modeling the throughput of TCP. A simplified version of the TCP throughput equation is given in RFC 5348 which defines the standard for TFRC. With a few variables set to recommended values, the equation for target transmit rate X in bits/sec is:

$$X = \frac{s}{R \times \sqrt{2p/3} + 12\sqrt{3p/8} \times p \times (1 + 32p^2)}$$

Where:

- s is the segment size (excluding IP and transport headers);

- R is the RTT in seconds;

- p is the number of "loss events" as a fraction of packets transmitted.

While the derivation of this formula is interesting in its own right (see the second reference below), the key idea here is that we have a pretty good idea of how much bandwidth a TCP connection will be able to deliver if we know the RTT and the loss rate of the path. So TFRC tries to steer applications that cannot implement a window-based congestion control algorithm to arrive at the same throughput as TCP would under the same conditions.

The only issues remaining to be addressed are the measurement of p and R, and then deciding how the application should respond to changes in X. Like some of the other protocols we have seen, TFRC uses timestamps to measure RTT more accurately than TCP originally did. Packet sequence numbers are used to determine packet loss at the receiver, with consecutive losses grouped into a single loss event. From this information the loss event rate p can be calculated at the receiver who then reflects it back to the sender.

Exactly how the application responds to a change in rate will of course depend on the application. The basic idea would be that an application can choose among a set of coding rates, and it picks the highest quality that can be accommodated with the rate that TFRC dictates.

While the concept of TFRC is solid, it has had limited deployment for a number of reasons. One is that a simpler solution for some types of streaming traffic emerged in the form of *DASH (Dynamic Adaptive Streaming over HTTP)*. DASH is only suitable for non-real-time media (e.g., watching movies) but that turns out to be a large percentage of the media traffic that runs across the Internet—in fact, it is a large percentage of *all* Internet traffic.

DASH lets TCP (or potentially QUIC) take care of congestion control; the application measures the throughput that TCP is delivering, then adjusts the quality of the video stream accordingly to avoid starvation at the receiver. This approach has proven to be suitable for video entertainment, but since it depends on a moderately large amount of buffering at the receiver to smooth out the fluctuations in TCP throughput, it is not really suitable for interactive audio or video. One of the key realizations that made DASH feasible was the idea that one could encode video at multiple quality levels with different bandwidth requirements, and store them all in advance on a streaming server. Then, as soon as the observed throughput of the network drops, the server can drop to a lower quality stream, and then ramp up to higher quality as conditions permit. The client can send information back to the server, such as how much buffered video it still has awaiting playback, to help the server choose a suitable quality and bandwidth stream. The cost of this approach is additional media storage on the server, but that cost has become rather unimportant in the modern streaming video era. Note that the "server" in this context is likely to be a node in a CDN (content distribution network). Hence, a video stream can take advantage of any improvement in the bandwidth available between a client and the CDN node serving it by shifting a higher quality level.

Another limitation of TFRC as defined is that it uses loss as its primary signal of congestion but does not respond to the delay that precedes loss. While this was the state of the art when work on TFRC was undertaken, the field of TCP congestion control has now moved on to take delay into account, as in the case of TCP Vegas and BBR (see Chapter 5). And this is particularly problematic when you consider that the class of multimedia applications that really need something other than DASH are precisely those applications for which delay is important. For this reason, work continues at the time of writing to define standards for TCP-friendly congestion control for real-time traffic. The IETF RMCAT (RTP Media Congestion Avoidance Techniques) working group is the home of this work. The specification of TFRC below therefore is not the final work, but gives useful background on how one might go about implementing a TCP-friendly protocol.

Further Reading:
S. Floyd, M. Handley, J. Padhye, and J. Widmer. TCP Friendly Rate Control (TFRC): Protocol Specification. RFC 5348, September 2008.

J. Padhye, V. Firoiu, D. Towsley, and J. Kurose. Modeling TCP Throughput: A Simple Model and its Empirical Validation. ACM SIGCOMM, September 1998.

7.5 Multipath Transport (MP-TCP)

While the early hosts connected to the Internet had only a single net-work interface, it is common these days to have interfaces to at least two different networks on a device. The most common example is a mobile phone with both cellular and WiFi interfaces. Another exam-ple is datacenters, which often allocate multiple network interfaces to servers to improve fault tolerance. Many applications use only one of the available networks at a time, but the potential exists to improve performance by using multiple interfaces simultaneously. This idea of multipath communication has been around for decades and led to a body of work at the IETF to standardize extensions to TCP to support end-to-end connections that leverage multiple paths between pairs of hosts. This is known as *Multipath TCP (MP-TCP)*.

A pair of hosts sending traffic over two or more paths simultane-ously has implications for congestion control. For example, if both paths share a common bottleneck link, then a naive implementation of one TCP connection per path would acquire twice as much share of the bottleneck bandwidth as a standard TCP connection. The de-signers of MPTCP set out to address this potential unfairness while also realizing the benefits of multiple paths. The proposed conges-tion control approach could equally be applied to other transports such as QUIC. The high level goals of congestion control for multipath transport are:

1. Perform at least as well as a single path flow on its best available path.

2. Do not take more resources from any path than a single path flow would take.

3. Move us much traffic as possible off the most congested path(s), consistent with the two preceding goals.

It's worth noting that the idea of fairness to other TCP flows has some subtleties, which we touched on in Section 3.2.

While the details involve complex bookkeeping, the overall ap-proach taken is straightforward. The congestion control algorithm roughly mimics that of TCP on a per-subflow basis, while trying to ensure that all three goals above are met. The core of the algorithm uses the following formula to increase the congestion window size of each individual subflow as ACKs are received on the subflow.

$$\text{MIN}\left(\frac{\alpha \times \text{BytesAcked} \times \text{MSS}_i}{\text{CongestionWindowTotal}}, \frac{\text{BytesAcked} \times \text{MSS}_i}{\text{CongestionWindow}_i}\right)$$

CongestionWindowTotal is the sum of congestion windows across all subflows, while CongestionWindow$_i$ is the congestion window of subflow i. The second argument to MIN mimics the increase that standard TCP would obtain, thus ensuring that the subflow is no more aggressive than TCP (goal 2). The first argument uses the variable α to ensure that, in aggregate, the multipath flow obtains the same throughput as it would have done using its best available path (goal 1). The calculation of α is described in detail in RFC 6356. Note that uncongested paths are able to grow their individual congestion windows more than congested paths as they do not suffer losses, and hence over time, more traffic moves onto the uncongested paths (goal 3).

While this is simple enough in retrospect, a lot of interesting analysis went into figuring out the right approach, as described in an NSDI paper by Wischik and colleagues.

7.6 Mobile Cellular Networks

We conclude with a use case that continues to attract attention from the research community: the interplay between congestion control and the mobile cellular network. Historically, the TCP/IP Internet and the mobile cellular network evolved independently, with the latter serving as the "last mile" for end-to-end TCP connections since the introduction of broadband service with 3G. With the rollout of 5G now ramping up, we can expect the mobile network will play an increasingly important role in providing Internet connectivity, putting increased focus on how it impacts congestion control.

While a mobile wireless connection could be viewed as no different than any other hop along an end-to-end path through the Internet,

Further Reading:
D. Wischik, C. Raiciu, A. Greenhalgh and M. Handley. Design, Implementation and Evaluation of Congestion Control for Multipath TCP. NSDI, April 2011.

C. Raiciu, M. Handley and D. Wischik. Coupled Congestion Control for Multipath Transport Protocols. RFC 6356, October 2011.

for historical reasons it has been treated as a special case, with the end-to-end path logically divided into the two segments depicted in Figure 42: the wired segment through the Internet and the wireless last-hop over the Radio Access Network (RAN). This "special case" perspective is warranted because (1) the wireless link is typically the bottleneck due to the scarcity of radio spectrum; (2) the bandwidth available in the RAN can be highly variable due to a combination of device mobility and radio interference; and (3) the number of devices being served by a given base station fluctuates as devices move from one cell to another.

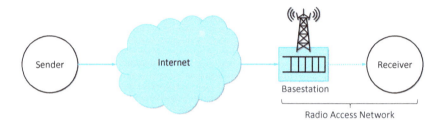

Figure 42: End-to-end path that includes a last-hop wireless link, where the base station buffers packets awaiting transmission over the Radio Access Network (RAN).

Although the internals of the RAN are largely closed and proprietary, researchers have experimentally observed that there is significant buffering at the edge, presumably to absorb the expected contention for the radio link, and yet keep sufficient work "close by" for whenever capacity does open up. As noted by Haiqing Jiang and colleagues in their 2012 CellNet workshop paper, this large buffer is problematic for TCP congestion control because it causes the sender to overshoot the actual bandwidth available on the radio link, and in the process, introduces significant delay and jitter. This is another example of the bufferbloat problem identified in Section 6.3.

The Jiang paper suggests possible solutions, and generally observes that delay-based approaches like Vegas outperform loss-based approaches like Reno or CUBIC, but the problem has remained largely unresolved for nearly a decade. With the promise of open source software-based implementations of the RAN now on the horizon (see our companion 5G and SDN books for more details), it might soon be possible to take a cross-layer approach, whereby the RAN provides an interface that give higher layers of the protocol stack (e.g., the

Further Reading:
H. Jiang, Z. Liu, Y. Wang, K. Lee and I. Rhee. Understanding Bufferbloat in Cellular Networks ACM SIGCOMM Workshop on Cellular Networks, August 2012.

AQM mechanisms described in Chapter 6) visibility into what goes on inside the base station. Recent research by Xie, Yi, and Jamieson suggests such an approach might prove effective, although their implementation uses end-device feedback instead of getting the RAN directly involved. How ever it's implemented, the idea is to have the receiver explicitly tell the sender how much bandwidth is available on the last hop, with the sender then having to judge whether the last-hop or some other point along the Internet segment is the actual bottleneck.

The other aspect of cellular networks that makes them a novel challenge for TCP congestion control is that the bandwidth of a link is not constant, but instead varies as a function of the signal-to-noise ratio experienced by each receiver. As noted by the BBR authors, the (currently opaque) scheduler for this wireless link can use the number of queued packets for a given client as an input to its scheduling algorithm, and hence the "reward" for building up a queue can be an increase in bandwidth provided by the scheduler. BBR has attempted to address this in its design by ensuring that it is aggressive enough to queue at least some packets in the buffers of wireless links.

Past research inquiries aside, it's interesting to ask if the wireless link will remain all that unique going forward. If you take a compartmentalized view of the world, and you're a mobile network operator, then your goal has historically been to maximize utilization of the scarce radio spectrum under widely varying conditions. Keeping the offered workload as high as possible, with deep queues, is a proven way to do that. This certainly made sense when broadband connectivity was the new service and voice and text were the dominant use cases, but today 5G is all about delivering good TCP performance. The focus should be on end-to-end goodput and maximizing the throughput/latency ratio (i.e., the power curve discussed in Section 3.2). But is there an opportunity for improvement?

We believe the answer to this question is yes. In addition to providing more visibility into the RAN scheduler and queues mentioned earlier, three other factors have the potential to change the equation. First, 5G deployments will likely support *network slicing*, a mechanism that isolates different classes of traffic. This means each slice has its

Further Reading:

Y. Xie, F. Yi, and K. Jamieson. PBE-CC: Congestion Control via Endpoint-Centric, Physical-Layer Bandwidth Measurements. SIGCOMM 2020.

L. Peterson and O. Sunay. 5G Mobile Networks: A Systems Approach. January 2020.

L. Peterson, C. Cascone, B. O'Connor, T. Vachuska, and B. Davie. Software-Defined Networks: A Systems Approach. November 2021.

own queue that can be sized and scheduled in a traffic-specific way. Second, the proliferation of *small cells* will likely reduce the number of flows competing for bandwidth at a given base station. How this impacts the scheduler's approach to maximizing spectrum utilization is yet to be seen. Third, it will become increasingly common for 5G-connected devices to be served from a nearby edge cloud rather than from the other side of the Internet. This means end-to-end TCP connections will have much shorter round-trip times, which will make the congestion control algorithm more responsive to changes in the available capacity in the RAN. There are no guarantees, of course, but all these factors should provide ample opportunities to tweak congestion control algorithms well into the future.

About The Book

Source for *TCP Congestion Control: A Systems Approach* is available on GitHub under terms of the Creative Commons (CC BY-NC-ND 4.0) license. The community is invited to contribute corrections, improvements, updates, and new material under the same terms. While this license does not automatically grant the right to make derivative works, we are keen to discuss derivative works (such as translations) with interested parties. Please reach out to discuss@systemsapproach.org.

If you make use of this work, the attribution should include the following information:

Title: TCP Congestion Control: A Systems Approach
Authors: Larry Peterson, Lawrence Brakmo, and Bruce Davie
Source: `https://github.com/SystemsApproach/tcpcc`
License: CC BY-NC-ND 4.0

Read the Book

This book is part of the Systems Approach Series, with an online version published at `https://tcpcc.systemsapproach.org`.

To track progress and receive notices about new versions, you can follow the project on Facebook and Twitter. To read a running commentary on how the Internet is evolving, subscribe to the Systems Approach newsletter on Substack.

Build the Book

To build a web-viewable version, you first need to download the source:

```
$ mkdir ~/tcpcc
$ cd ~/tcpcc
$ git clone https://github.com/SystemsApproach/tcpcc.git
```

The build process is stored in the Makefile and requires Python be installed. The Makefile will create a virtualenv (venv-docs) which installs the documentation generation toolset. You may also need to install the enchant C library using your system's package manager for the spelling checker to function properly.

To generate HTML in _build/html, run make html.

To check the formatting of the book, run make lint.

To check spelling, run make spelling. If there are additional words, names, or acronyms that are correctly spelled but not in the dictionary, please add them to the dict.txt file.

To see the other available output formats, run make.

Contribute to the Book

We hope that if you use this material, you are also willing to contribute back to it. If you are new to open source, you might check out this How to Contribute to Open Source guide. Among other things, you'll learn about posting *Issues* that you'd like to see addressed, and issuing *Pull Requests* to merge your improvements back into GitHub.

If you'd like to contribute and are looking for something that needs attention, see the wiki for the current TODO list.

About The Authors

Larry Peterson is the Robert E. Kahn Professor of Computer Science, Emeritus at Princeton University, where he served as Chair from 2003-2009. His research focuses on the design, implementation, and operation of Internet-scale distributed systems, including the widely used PlanetLab and MeasurementLab platforms. He is currently contributing to the Aether access-edge cloud project at the Open Networking Foundation (ONF), where he serves as Chief Scientist. Peterson is a member of the National Academy of Engineering, a Fellow of the ACM and the IEEE, the 2010 recipient of the IEEE Kobayashi Computer and Communication Award, and the 2013 recipient of the ACM SIGCOMM Award. He received his Ph.D. degree from Purdue University.

Lawrence Brakmo currently works in the Kernel group at Facebook. Prior to joining Facebook, he was a member of the Host Networking group at Google, and before that, a researcher and project manager of the OS group at DoCoMo USA Labs. Brakmo has worked on TCP enhancements to improve network performance, including the design of the TCP Vegas and TCP-NV congestion control algorithms. He has also developed OS techniques to improve system reliability, performance, and energy consumption. Brakmo received his Ph.D. degree in Computer Science from The University of Arizona.

Bruce Davie is a computer scientist noted for his contributions to the field of networking. He is a former VP and CTO for the Asia Pacific region at VMware. He joined VMware during the acquisition of Software Defined Networking (SDN) startup Nicira. Prior to that, he was a Fellow at Cisco Systems, leading a team of architects responsible for Multiprotocol Label Switching (MPLS). Davie has over 30 years of networking industry experience and has co-authored 17 RFCs. He was recognized as an ACM Fellow in 2009 and chaired ACM SIGCOMM from 2009 to 2013. He was also a visiting lecturer at the Massachusetts Institute of Technology for five years. Davie is the author of multiple books and the holder of more than 40 U.S. Patents.

www.ingramcontent.com/pod-product-compliance
Lightning Source LLC
Chambersburg PA
CBHW040217090326
40690CB00065B/5286